# WHAT
# WOMEN

## WANT
## COACHES TO
## KNOW

# ENDORSEMENTS

Rosieda Shabodien generously gifts us with a book fit for purpose to transform the world of work as we know it, while keeping gender equality, diversity, and inclusion central. Drawing from an intersectional perspective, the book surfaces the ubiquitous nature of gender bias and sexism and makes a compelling argument for why coaches and organisations should adopt a gender-intelligent approach to coaching.

*Sixolile Ngcobo, Director: The Well Health Company;*
*Director: NSP GBVF Localisation at The World of Impact*

An urgently required and timely authoritative guide on gender-intelligent coaching, which is an innovative and inclusive methodology, that recognises and addresses the complexities of different gender dynamics in coaching relationships, and seeks to combat the impacts of sexism and racism on society.

This book is a bold, dynamic, transformative publication, designed to address the unique and systemic challenges of gender discrimination, and explores potential challenges that women face in their personal and professional lives. Women-centric coaching recognises the necessity of creating safe spaces for women to explore their dreams, hopes, goals, and purpose. It captures the diverse experiences, opinions, strengths, perspectives and incredible value that women bring, it celebrates their journeys and stories so that they might progress and inspire and uplift others.

Through this women-centric coaching approach, women are encouraged to embrace their authentic selves, pursue self-discovery, build confidence, overcome self-doubt, embrace their potential, and develop skills necessary to navigate a complex world.

Women-centred coaching paves the way for reflection, growth, career advancement, and personal fulfilment. It fosters a sense of community, empathy, trust, belonging, connectedness and understanding.

I salute the author for her bold leadership and courage.

*Dr Shirley Zinn, Chair and Independent Non-Executive Board Director: Sanlam, MTN (SA), VNA, Spur Corporation and Spar Group*

Rosieda invites readers on a transformative voyage through the world of coaching. With a blend of eloquence and insight, she skilfully navigates the complexities of becoming a coach while addressing critical societal challenges. Her writing style is a breath of fresh air. She effortlessly weaves metaphors, analogies, and everyday quirks into her narrative, making the book an accessible and enjoyable read. Her personal journey—from activist to master's student to coach—shines through, providing honest glimpses into her experiences.

The heart of her book lies in its exploration of the watershed moments that lead individuals to seek coaching. Through vivid storytelling, Rosieda captures the essence of these pivotal moments, emphasising that seeking a coach is not a decision to be taken lightly. It's a journey of self-discovery and growth. The book fearlessly confronts the formidable challenge posed by patriarchal norms. By integrating well-known theories with her own coaching model, she empowers female coaching clients to understand how societal constructs shape their experiences.

Coaches too, gain critical awareness, ensuring they don't fall prey to denialism or substitution when addressing social contexts. Rosieda's commitment to her own deep reflective analysis sets this book apart. She encourages readers to engage with their own reflections and insights, fostering a thoughtful approach to coaching.

Whether you're a seasoned coach or someone curious about the field, this book offers valuable insights. It's a must-read for anyone passionate about equality, personal growth, and the art of coaching. It's a beacon guiding us toward a more empowered and understanding world.

*Sonya Van Wyk, Learning & Development Consultant & Coach*

This book is like a GPS to our hidden biases and assumptions. Rosieda's wisdom and expertise create a powerful guide to navigating blind spots in the workplace and ourselves. It is an invaluable tool for coaches, business women, managers, and policymakers!

*Prof Krista Tuomi, Professor and*
*Entrepreneurial Finance Specialist*

Rosieda's book, "What Women Want Coaches to Know: The Gender-Intelligent Coaching Approach," breaks new ground in offering a fresh perspective on gender-aware transformational coaching. This is not just a coaching book. It is a call to all of us to awaken to the deeper yearning within humanity to be more than inclusive. It is an invitation to be more humane. Dive into it with an open mind and expect to be challenged, enlightened and inspired.

*Dr Dumisani Magadlela, Executive Coach (PCC) and*
*Author of best-selling book "Ubuntu Coaching and*
*Connection Practices for Leader Managers"*

"What Women Want Coaches to Know: A Gender-Intelligent Coaching Approach" is a piece of work that broadens the discourse on coaching by integrating gender awareness into the practice. Through six insightful chapters, it addresses the unique challenges women face, advocating for a transformative coaching approach that empowers women and fosters gender equality. This book is a must-read for coaches committed to creating inclusive environments and driving systemic change. It not only offers practical strategies but also inspires reflection and action towards a more equitable world, making it an invaluable addition to the literature on coaching and women's empowerment.

*Prof J Frantz, Deputy Vice Chancellor: Research and Innovation,*
*University of Western Cape*

As a woman leader in the non-profit sector, this is the companion I am looking for to help me find my transformative power and create the organisation that enables others to find theirs. Rosieda's offering is insightful, completely relatable and wonderfully quirky at times.

*Miriam van Donk, Director: Isandla Institute*

First published in 2024.

ISBN: 978-1-991272-13-3
eISBN: 978-1-991272-14-0

Published by KR Publishing
Tel: (011) 706-6009
E-mail: orders@knowres.co.za
Website: www.kr.co.za

**Printed and bound:** INGRAM Lightning Source
**Typesetting, layout and design:** Cia Joubert, cia@knowres.co.za
**Cover design:** Marlene De Lorme, marlene@knowres.co.za
**Editing & proofreading:** KR Publishing & Nasreen Variyawa
**Project management:** Cia Joubert, cia@knowres.co.za

# WHAT
# WOMEN
# WANT
# COACHES TO
# KNOW

by

## Rosieda Shabodien

**kr**
publishing

2024

# ACKNOWLEDGEMENTS

I am deeply grateful for the privilege of being published by KR Publishing. Wilhelm Crous and Cia Joubert provided unwavering support from inception to completion, guiding me through challenges and setbacks, including a two-month health crisis where the book had to take a backseat. Their invaluable guidance steered me through the authoring process, and I am thankful for the opportunity to share my work through such a distinguished publishing house.

While I am the sole author, Nasreen Variyawa, Director of Nasreeniology, played a crucial role as the book "doula." I am deeply grateful for your extensive editorial support and ongoing encouragement to bring this book to life.

I am immensely grateful to have a tribe of supportive friends. Expansive gratitude to dearest friends Edgar Pieterse, Mirjam van Donk, Chi-wah Chan and Krista Tuomi, who did not once roll their eyes when I nagged about *The Coaching Book.* I am also indebted to friends and coaches who generously gifted their time and expertise—Niamaat Gamildien, Krista Tuomi, Sonya van Wyk, Andre Blaauw, and Janice Hanly —thank you for your thoughtful engagement and constructive criticism. Appreciation, Caroline Dale, for your advice on contacting KR Publishing. Tons of appreciation, Layla Williams of Elite Desk; your superb admin and project support was invaluable.

To my women coaching clients: You are already brilliant, and it is a profound honour to serve as your coach!

To the Shabodien and Rasool clans: You keep me real and make me who I am! Shukran for your constant support and encouragement in achieving my life goals.

To my children—Tahrir, Sanjay, and Tanwir—you are the heartbeats of my life. Your presence in my life is an ongoing blessing! Your steadfast support, sprinkled with words of encouragement, teasing, and laughter, has been a source of motivation throughout the writing of this book. Sanjay and Tahrir so much, Shukr for rescuing me from my reference nightmare!

Living with someone who grapples with imposter syndrome, is an introvert at heart and has fluctuating dopamine levels, undoubtedly presents its challenges. My beloved Ebrahim, partner, spouse, and best friend, lives with *that* someone. I am deeply grateful for your support on this book journey, especially when my confidence wavered, and my writing legs became unsteady. I am indebted to you for being my sentient being, my alpenglow, and my forever companion on this adventurous journey we call life.

Most importantly, I praise the Almighty (SWT), who is the ultimate planner of my life, and for this, I'm grateful.

# TABLE OF CONTENTS

# ABOUT THE AUTHOR

***Rosieda Shabodien*** is a black South African woman who is deeply committed to creating a world where every person is given the opportunity to achieve their highest ideals and potential while remaining abloom on the path of ongoing self-transcendence.

Born during apartheid in an impoverished yet vibrant community in Cape Town, on the Cape Flats, she recounts her birth story, where the midwife swaddled her in a newspaper. She believes the newspaper's words seeped into her, igniting her passion for seeking knowledge, looking beyond the headlines, and unearthing the complex stories beneath.

Rosieda lives by the dictum that while we cannot choose where or to whom we are born, we have the power to shape our destiny through our actions.

She joined the anti-apartheid struggle at the age of fourteen, setting her on a lifelong trajectory to work for human rights and societal transformation. She has held various leadership positions in human rights and women's advocacy organisations. She is well-known for her advocacy for gender equality and women's rights, playing a central role in developing South Africa's legislation on equal gender representation in parliament and local government and advocating for legislation that creates a gender-just society.

In her pursuit of women's empowerment and human development, Rosieda embraced coaching as a powerful tool for cultivating empowerment. She obtained a Master's in Management Coaching from Stellenbosch University, completed a professional training course in Coaching to Excellence and an associate coaching course at the Centre for Coaching in Cape Town. Additionally, she holds a degree in Physiotherapy from the University of the Western Cape. She adopted the gender-intelligent coaching approach to coach women and men to overcome limiting beliefs and biases. She specialises in coaching women leaders, empowering them to lead with brilliance and authenticity.

Over the past 15 years, her innovative coaching work has sparked profound transformations in individuals, teams, and organisations across diverse sectors, including NPOs, academia, and social entrepreneurship. Rosieda has an exceptional talent for coaching her clients to unearth profound self-knowledge, igniting the courage to change and pursue their unfolding life stories shaped by the values they hold and the actions they take.

Rosieda wrote "What Women Want Coaches to Know: The Gender-Intelligent Coaching Approach," inspired by Nobel laureate Toni Morrison's words, "If there's a book that you want to read but it hasn't been written yet, then you must write it".

# GLOSSARY

| Term | Definition |
| --- | --- |
| Gender | Gender refers to the socially constructed roles, behaviours, and expectations associated with being male or female in a society. While sex is biological, gender roles are societal expectations of men and women. To illustrate this point, consider the widespread cultural expectation that women should primarily tend to the needs of their families and do domestic duties. The traditional view holds that men should be the primary breadwinners and not be involved in caring for their families or doing housework, but rather should focus on providing financial support for their families. |
| Gender Bias | Gender bias refers to unfair and prejudiced attitudes, behaviours, and actions towards individuals based on their sex, negatively impacting both men and women. However, women often bear the brunt of gender bias. This bias is evident when a male colleague receives a promotion over a woman, despite her equal or superior qualifications, due to the perception that women are not suited for leadership roles or receive biased evaluations compared to their male counterparts. |
| Gender Stereotypes | Gender stereotypes are overly simplified and rigid *beliefs* about men's and women's characteristics, traits, and behaviours based on societal norms. For instance, a common stereotype is women are more emotional and nurturing than men. This stereotype equates emotionality with a lack of assertiveness, leading to women being overlooked for leadership roles that require assertiveness. |

| Term | Definition |
|---|---|
| Intersectionality | As a conceptual framework, intersectionality reflects the ways in which marginalised people confront compounded biases due to the interconnected nature of many forms of inequality, such as gender, class, and race. An example of intersectionality in the workforce could be a black woman facing both race and gender discrimination, which can lead to reduced opportunities for career advancement compared to her white and black male colleagues. |
| Misogyny | Patriarchy describes a fundamental enmity or hostility towards women. An example of misogyny in the workplace could be a male supervisor, out of his innate disregard for women, consistently ignoring or dismissing the ideas and contributions of female employees. This attitude can create a toxic work environment for women, hindering their professional growth and reinforcing gender discrimination. |
| Patriarchy | As a political and social system, patriarchy promotes men at the cost of women, by advancing men as the principal holders of power and authority in political, state, economic, religious, and cultural spheres. Patriarchal societies, for example, may systematically exclude women from leadership positions in government, thereby limiting their ability to influence decision-making and shape policies that impact their lives. |

| Term | Definition |
|------|------------|
| Prejudice | To be prejudiced is to hold a preconceived negative view and attitude towards an individual or group because of their actual difference from one's own race, sex, religion, social orientation, ethnicity, or other social identities. For example, there are discriminatory impediments to women's advancement in STEM (science, technology, engineering, and mathematics) professions due to the widespread belief that men are more qualified for these roles and the erroneous belief that women are less capable in STEM roles. |
| Racism | Racism is characterised by deeply ingrained systemic and individual bias and discrimination against a marginalised racial group, particularly individuals of colour, resulting in differences and imbalances in treatment, conduct, opportunities, and resource distribution. An example of racism in the workforce could be a company consistently passing qualified black candidates for promotions in favour of less qualified white candidates, reinforcing the belief that certain racial groups are inherently less capable. |
| Sex | Sex refers to a person's unique set of biological, physiological and physical traits that distinguish males and females, such as their chromosomes and reproductive organs, among others. |
| Sexism | Sexism is defined as discrimination or bias based on an individual's sex, specifically against women, as well as systematic inequitable treatment, preconceived notions, and prejudice across numerous social, economic, and political spheres. For example, women may receive less favourable performance evaluations compared to their male counterparts, even when there is no difference in the quality of their output because there is a belief that men are more suited for specific work roles. |

# INTRODUCTION:
# COACHING WOMEN TO NAVIGATE
# THE PATRIARCHAL RIVERS

*"I long to speak about the intense inspiration that comes to me from the lives of strong women. They have made their lives a great adventure."*

Ruth Benedict
(Anthropologist and Folklorist)

I obtained my Master's Degree in Coaching from Stellenbosch University in 2020. However, the COVID pandemic rained on my parade since that dangerous and sneaky virus forced the world and the university into lockdown. That meant I could not, as I envisioned, strut across the graduation stage with my master's certificate in hand, to show the "world," aka my family and friends, that I had finally achieved my master's degree.

Accordingly, the master's certificate was unceremoniously mailed to me. While I could not do the "look-how-clever-I-am" graduation parade I had anticipated, the master's certificate proudly adorns our home's celebration stand.

Beyond being delighted to have graduated, I was particularly thrilled with my postgrad status, considering this was not my first attempt at a master's degree. Allow me to share a little secret with you: many moons ago, I attempted a Master's in Epidemiology. Yes, I could have been an expert on navigating the twists and turns of the COVID-19 pandemic. Although I successfully completed the coursework, the elusive thesis remained unfinished, leaving me without the official title. My justifications at the time for not completing the thesis were convincing, which included that the demands of balancing work in both the health, gender and women's development sectors left me with little bandwidth to devote time to my thesis. Ultimately, I made a deliberate choice to prioritise my commitment to advancing gender equality, leading to a pivot away from epidemiology.

Simultaneously, I had just become a first-time mother. However, it would be grossly inaccurate if I were to paint the sacrificial narrative where I alone shouldered the responsibility of being the primary child carer, cook and cleaner, as so often expected of women. I was fortunate, given the fact my spouse and I established a marriage template consistent with our commitment to gender equality principles and values, which then practically entailed the equitably shared responsibility for childcare, household chores, and cooking. In other words, we were both full-time working individuals; therefore, all childcare, caring, domestic cleaning, and cooking were equally apportioned between us. This equitable division was not only about fairness and practicality but also our deep commitment to justice and debunking the archaic roles assigned to men and women and the straight-jacketing of women into dominant roles of caring, cleaning and cooking and men into the breadwinner's roles.

Nevertheless, time juggling between motherhood, spousehood, extended family connections and engagements, pursuing my career, and engaging in political activism, proved to be a formidable challenge.

Adding to the complexity of my life's tapestry, my beloved South Africa was undergoing a monumental transition from the oppressive apartheid regime to a nascent democracy. As an anti-apartheid activist deeply committed to non-racialism and democracy, as well as advancing gender equality and women's empowerment, I recognised this as a pivotal moment to embed these ideals into the slew of new laws and policies in post-apartheid and democratic South Africa.

Thus, I accepted the directorship of a gender advocacy and lobbying organisation and was subsequently appointed Commissioner at South Africa's Commission for Gender Equality. I, therefore, made a deliberate choice to focus my efforts on driving the gender equality movement forward.

With such lofty responsibilities, neither university peers, family, nor friends could contest the reasons I had neatly lined up for shelving my epidemiology master's degree. It was accepted that the significant progress I could make in advancing gender equality outweighed the need to complete my degree—even I believed that story!

Fast-forward to 2011. The spectre of the incomplete master's degree secretly lived in the republic of regret. There I was in Washington, DC, in the US, on one of those picturesque snowy days; I found myself absentmindedly perusing through a book, "The Secret Thoughts of Highly Effective Women", authored by Valerie Young[1].

Little did I anticipate the profound impact it would have on me, and without sounding too dramatic, it brought about what I call my "watershed moment". Up to that present moment, I had never encountered the concept of *imposter syndrome*. This book was a game-changer for me since I was not just experiencing a smattering of lightbulb moments, but my brain lit up like a Christmas tree. I finally knew what was ailing me.

Young revealed that people suffering from imposter syndrome are trapped in a dominant belief that one's success and accomplishments are only due to good fortune as opposed to intelligence, wisdom, experience and super hard work. She articulates that the imposter syndrome is when "...people who have a persistent belief in their *lack* of intelligence, skills, or competence ... are convinced that other people's praise and recognition of their accomplishments is undeserved, chalking up their achievements to chance, charm, connections, and other external factors. Unable to internalise or feel deserving of their success, they continue to doubt their ability to repeat past successes"[2].

Young built on the ground-breaking research on the imposter phenomenon conducted by Dr Pauline Clance and Dr Suzanne Imes[3]. Their findings shed light on the imposter phenomenon prevalent among high-achieving individuals. Not surprisingly, their study revealed that although both men and women grapple with imposter syndrome, women were significantly more likely to suffer from it. Their findings also highlighted the profound psychological toll of imposter syndrome on high-achieving women, who constantly felt as if they were masquerading as accomplished individuals; all the while fearing that someday they would be exposed as frauds, their façade ripped away, and their 'true' incompetence revealed.

The burden of imposter syndrome weighs heavily on those who grapple with it, sowing seeds of doubt, fear, and self-loathing that stifle the pursuit of new successes, replicating past triumphs, and just ongoing hard slogging. Can you fathom the relentless psychological stress that accompanies such self-doubt and ambivalence?

As Young's words washed over me, I felt a profound sense of resonance—someone had actually revealed the emotions that lived within me, hindering my journey towards self-actualisation. In this moment of clarity, a moment of healing—my heart ached as I reflected on the younger versions of myself, the young teenage girl, the young woman, and now the adult woman—who constantly evaded the spotlight, shying away from leadership and acclamation, haunted by the sheer terror of being unmasked as an imposter, a fraud who feigned her intelligence.

But the journey to overcoming the debilitating imposter syndrome does not rest on a single epiphany; it requires a series of insights. In my case, four pivotal insights reshaped my path forward.

The first insight was that my decision to abandon my master's degree was indeed rooted in negative self-perception and deep-seated self-doubt, fuelled by self-sabotage. I realised the reason why my epidemiology master's journey was so joyless, so fearful-laden—a veritable rollercoaster ride from aspiration to feeling undeserving of the title *epidemiologist*. Thus, I pressed the eject button and abandoned the master's degree.

The second insight, only visible from the front-row seat of my life, revealed a landscape littered with opportunities I had rejected, all the offers I had shrunk away from, and all the abandoned endeavours. I surveyed the wasteland of self-sabotage and recognised how my imposter syndrome dimmed my light, limited my horizons, cast a shadow on my accomplishments, and deprived me of the enjoyment of my work. It was a debilitating cycle, filled with angst and doubt, that cost me years of well-deserved recognition for the work that I have done and was passionate about.

My third realisation was born out of understanding the impact of imposter syndrome, and notwithstanding my accomplishments, I felt a profound sense of regret. I lamented that I had treated myself unjustly—the toll of carrying the dual burden of striving to excel while simultaneously working relentlessly just to ensure people didn't think of me as I thought of myself—being unworthy and a fraud! It dawned on me that what I was doing was akin to running marathon after marathon, only to spurn the medal at the finish line!

Lastly, I came to realise that something so life-negating as imposter syndrome cannot merely be a single phenomenon that predominantly impacts women; it must surely be part of a whole host of phenomena affecting women. It unquestionably must have accomplices. This led me to ponder why, despite working for most of my adult life in the gender and women's empowerment sector, completing an associate coaching course, participating and presenting at local and global women's and gender seminars, workshops and conferences—did imposter syndrome never come up as a consideration in these sectors?

Motivated by a desire to understand why the concept of imposter syndrome remained relatively obscure to me, I embarked on an intellectual journey to explore the phenomenon and whether there were any similar conditions and concepts impacting women's lives. My research revealed a startling revelation: imposter syndrome is merely one among a constellation of challenges affecting women's well-being and self-actualisation journeys. Why do these challenges persist among women? All fingers were pointed at patriarchy—a powerful political and social system that dictates that if you are born male, you are automatically assigned to exercise power and control by dominating leadership roles in social, political, and economic systems, and assigning men the prerogative to define moral authority, social privilege, women's status, and women's rights.

It dawned on me that we often underestimate the profound negative impact "father patriarchy" and his offspring—misogyny and sexism—have on the fundamental fabric of both women's and men's lives. What surprised me even more was my realisation that despite my deep work in women's empowerment and gender equality and my self-identification as a womanist and gender-equity specialist, thus fully immersed in the patriarchal discourse and its negative impact on men and women, I still, despite all this knowledge, to some extent underestimated the malevolent effects of systemic patriarchy.

This realisation prompted me to re-evaluate how I coach women. It dawned on me that when we coach women, we cannot ignore the unique challenges they face due to their biological sex, being born female, and the prevailing social gender norms that discriminate against females and favour males. Recognising that patriarchy is still deeply entrenched in our societies necessitates that we not simply treat the gendered challenges women face as unexpected hurdles in unfamiliar territory. Instead, as coaches, we must acknowledge what women encounter is a familiar patriarchal minefield in both their private and professional lives and it is not just unfamiliar territory but should be regarded as hostile territory.

However, if we disregard the patriarchal environment and the impact it has on women, it would be like instructing a swimmer to cross a river but alarmingly, withholding a vital piece of information: the river is crocodile-infested! Astonishingly, this parallels how we coach women without acknowledging the pervasive influence of patriarchy—a force that thwarts women's loftiest aspirations.

Similarly, coaching should not solely focus on boosting the innate talent and brilliance of our women clients while ignoring the patriarchal context in which they operate. For example, a woman leader may possess exceptional leadership qualities but face gender biases and discrimination and barriers at work, making it difficult to advance in her career. Effective coaching must involve both developing her leadership skills and inspiring her to create strategies to navigate systemic challenges. Unfortunately, coaches often concentrate on enhancing women's leadership presence, skills, and voice but neglect to coach them in strategies to prepare them for the systemic gendered environment they face. This approach is analogous to training a swimmer to perfect her technique and boost her endurance without warning her about the crocodiles lurking in the river.

Moreover, women are often unfairly accused of lacking the resilience to withstand a gender-biased work environment. This is equivalent to blaming a swimmer for being attacked by crocodiles because she hasn't perfected her technique or isn't strong or fast enough. Regardless of the swimmer's strength, stroke, or determination, the odds are stacked against her in a crocodile-infested river. Hence, it is naïve to expect sheer talent and courage will protect her from the dangers posed by the crocodiles.

The critical question that arises in the coaching profession is this: what is the role of the coaching profession when faced with social and political complexity? This book, "A Gender-Intelligent Coaching Approach", specifically delves into the question of how we coach women who find themselves in an oppressive context and experience discrimination based not only on their biological sex but also on race and ethnicity.

Now I hear the drums beating in sync with the assertion that "coaching and coaches are neutral agents!" This book's central thesis of inquiry is that we must complexify the notion of neutrality in coaching since, often under the guise of so-called neutrality, we might inadvertently perpetuate and support dominant social ideologies[4].

Furthermore, the approach to coaching women should not solely be based on a "fix-the-women" perspective but rather fix the system that gives rise to the gendered nature of problems women are encountering[5]. Simply coaching women to boost their talent and brilliance while turning a blind eye to the patriarchal barriers they face overlooks the potentiality of coaching. Effective coaching should empower women to develop strategies to navigate the women-specific and gendered challenges they face.

Moreover, I realised simply being aware of the presence of crocodiles in a river does not suffice; one must still cross the river. The question confronting me then was, "How can coaching assist women to navigate the 'patriarchal' river?" This pressing question fuelled my desire to pursue a master's degree in executive coaching, armed with this burning question and, this time, with greater self-belief in my abilities. I also vowed the song of doubt would not awaken the imposter syndrome that haunted me during my previous master's degree.

I embarked on a quest to explore how coaching, the hottest new kid in the human potential and human development arena, could be impactful in assisting women to unearth their strengths, talents, and skills. The goal was to ensure women create a powerful presence despite the pervasive influence of systemic patriarchy. Critically, I sought a coaching approach that intentionally coach women to navigate patriarchal and sexist systems. This coaching approach would assist them to reclaim and enhance their inner psyche, strengths, talents, and skills, and empower them to address discrimination and biases head-on.

This time, I approached my coaching master's degree pursuit with a fresh perspective. I donned a new pair of lenses enriched by previous insights and viewed everything through the prism of gender. I scrutinised lectures, prescribed coaching literature and reading materials, coaching models, and theories with gendered awareness. My research into patriarchy and its impact on women, combined with my experience in coaching women, enriched this perspective. I analysed coaching frameworks, coaching models, and coaching tools to see how they might have a different impact on women. I also meticulously assessed gender bias in the coaching approaches—prejudiced actions or thoughts based on the perception that women are not equal to men or as worthy as men. Additionally, I evaluated the assumed neutrality of these coaching approaches. For instance, when reviewing coaching interventions for time management, I scrutinised whether they catered solely to men, women, or both, and whether they considered the social contexts in which women operate.

Next, the gender representation of the lecturers of the master's coaching course drew my attention. Diverse gender and race representation brings diverse perspectives, yet most of the lectures were delivered by white men, closely followed by white women, with only a scattering of black men and women. This struck me as paradoxical since the coaching fraternity currently consists predominantly of women coaches. Additionally, most of the prescribed coaching books were authored by men. Of course, women authors were also included in the prescribed literature, but most books distributed to the master's cohort were from male authors. It was particularly insightful to read two prescribed books by two coaching authors, one male and one female, who took up the issue of diversity considerations in coaching, with a particular focus on coaching women in gender-biased work settings[6].

In addition, I noticed a glaring oversight: the failure to acknowledge the powerful detrimental impact racism and institutional patriarchy have on human achievement. This oversight I found strikingly ironic, given the emphasis on coaching interventions being sensitive to our clients' contextual nuances. It was even more remarkable, considering this omission occurred in my master's coaching curriculum in South Africa, a country where the legacy of apartheid is still profoundly felt. This realisation underscored a critical point. If the coaching profession wants to be regarded as a formidable profession in enhancing human capacity, it must engage in discourses about how coaching interventions must consider the context. Specifically, it must take into account the prejudiced and discriminatory environments some of our coaching clients, particularly women, have to navigate daily in their private as well as professional lives.

As a result of all these reflections, I concluded that my dissertation ought to address the pivotal inquiry, "What is the perceived value of coaching for women in the non-profit sector?"

Existing research findings confirmed that women who received coaching reported its positive impact[8]. However, I aimed to delve deeper into *how* coaching specifically made a positive impact on women and identify areas where we could improve the coaching experience for women. While I could have posed this research question to women across various industries, I intentionally narrowed my focus to the non-profit organisation (NPO) sector for several reasons:

- Due to constraints on time and resources to conduct the research, focusing on a single sector allowed for a more in-depth exploration. Additionally, given my work in the NPO sector, I anticipated minimal issues in accessing the targeted research population.

- Despite the predominance of women leaders in the NPO sector, their perspectives remain largely neglected in coaching research, and it was imperative to amplify their voices within the body of coaching research.

- My research focused on *working* women to reflect the reality of women globally—women form a critical part of the workforce!

Although my research specifically targeted women leaders in the NPO sector, the findings have broader implications for working women across all sectors. Notably, the study revealed that some women encountered gender biases in their work environments. Importantly, when the assigned coach demonstrated an understanding of gender issues, these women leaders utilised the coaching space to address and navigate these gendered challenges. However, when coaches were oblivious to gender dynamics, the concerns raised by their female clients about gender-based challenges were often overlooked as pressing coaching issues.

These research findings sparked a desire to continue exploring how coaching can integrate a gender mainstreaming perspective, particularly when we coach women who endure the brunt of gender bias. Several distinct questions guided my research journey:

1. What is the current gendered landscape, and what are the unique challenges working women face, particularly in terms of gendered bias and gender stereotypes?

2. Has the coaching landscape embraced diversity and considered the power dynamics regarding gender, race, and ethnicity?

3. Does the coaching profession treat coaching as a neutral modality, or can coaching serve as a tool for change in challenging social contexts?

4. Which coaching frameworks and coaching models are best suited for coaching women, and is there a need to develop unique coaching frameworks and models for women?

5. If our women coaching clients were to communicate directly with coaches, what would they express regarding their expectations of coaches and coaching?

6. Lastly, what will it take to construct a gender-intelligent coaching approach?

To me, these questions were not just academic; they formed the blueprint for transforming coaching into a force for gender equity.

Embarking on this intellectual journey to answer these questions, I felt inspired and compelled to engage in dialogue and share my findings, insights, musings, and reflections. "What better vessel for this discourse than a book?" I pondered. All I can say is, be cautious about your ponderings because this book, "What Women Want Coaches to Know - A Gender-Intelligent Coaching Approach," emerged from my contemplations.

Writing this book was not easy. When you write your first book, you tend to burden it with all your knowledge on a particular topic. However, to maintain self-control, I made a deal with myself. I'll only write about my real-life coaching experience with the gender-intelligent coaching approach. I have also coached men using the gender-intelligent coaching approach, but I may save that for my next book. This book focuses on coaching women living in a patriarchal world, which probably applies to 99.9 percent of women.

# OVERVIEW

Ultimately, the essence of this book, "What Women Want Coaches to Know: A Gender-Intelligent Coaching Approach," lies in its aim to contribute to the growing body of literature on the coaching process, particularly broadening the coaching discourse regarding its role in fostering gender transformation and women's empowerment. Within its pages, six chapters weave a tapestry of why adopting a gender-intelligent coaching approach is important, and each chapter sheds light on crucial aspects of coaching women from a gendered perspective.

While the focus within these pages is on the gender-intelligent coaching approach, the broader aspiration remains fostering a more inclusive and equitable world for all. It is also my hope that reading this book will ignite reflection regarding your coaching approach in the context of the pervasive influence of biases and prejudices based on gender and race in society. Perhaps this book will also spark a drive in you to take up the challenge and write your own coaching book based on your coaching experience. However, first, I invite you to read my offerings to you and invite all coaches to join me on this inspiring journey of being dedicated to ongoing learning, unlearning, and creating spaces that empower individuals to thrive beyond the constraints of societal prejudices. Together, we can elevate the coaching profession into a globally transformative force for good, especially in women's lives everywhere.

Now, let's explore how the gender-intelligent coaching approach can best serve women.

**Chapter One:** A Festival of Metaphors - A Litany of Discrimination

In chapter one, we embark on an exploration of patriarchy's pervasive influence and its negative impact on working women specifically. The chapter also highlights the "think leader, think male" phenomenon and how historical male dominance has perpetuated patriarchal views, sidelining women and minorities in leadership.

The chapter also acknowledges the emotional intensity surrounding gender equality and women's empowerment. It assists the reader in transitioning from feelings to facts by using vivid metaphors to illustrate the undeniable repercussions of patriarchy and the pervasive impact of sexism and gender bias. Additionally, the chapter delves into the intersectionality of racism and sexism, showing how these intertwined biases affect marginalised groups. By exploring these concepts and metaphors, the chapter sets the stage for understanding the importance of adopting a gender-intelligent coaching approach.

**Chapter Two:** Coaching for Diversity, Equality, and Inclusion

This chapter comprehensively explores the need for diversity, equality, and inclusion within the coaching profession, emphasising the transformative potential of gender-intelligent coaching in creating a more equitable world.

This chapter explores the burgeoning field of coaching, particularly its critical role in promoting diversity, equality, and inclusion. It begins by focusing on the current coaching landscape and addressing the profession's dual challenges in defining what coaching is and determining who qualifies as a coach.

It then delves into the proliferation of coaching specialisations and outlines the foundational values of coaching. It also traces the origins of the coaching profession, noting its rapid growth and evolution. The chapter concludes by reiterating the importance of gender-intelligent coaching for individual empowerment, women's empowerment, systemic change, and fostering an equitable and thriving society.

**Chapter Three:** Painting the Canvas for a Gender-Intelligent Coaching Approach

Chapter three dives into the development of the gender-intelligent coaching approach. It begins by establishing the core coaching values that underpin this approach, setting a foundation for a practice focused on facilitating self-exploration and awakening the brilliance within clients, ensuring the best possible coaching experience.

The chapter also clarifies essential coaching terminology, differentiating between a coaching framework, coaching model, and coaching tools. It emphasises the importance of understanding this coaching lingo to develop a sound and effective approach. The development and integration of these elements are illustrated through practical examples, such as the analogy of supporting a client across a bridge on her journey from her current-reality to her desired-reality.

The chapter also details the creation of the gender-intelligent coaching approach, demonstrating the integration of selected theories and paradigms to address the gender-specific challenges women encounter and discusses the practical application of coaching models to efficiently support clients in achieving their desired outcomes.

**Chapter Four:** The Language of the W-O-M-A-N Coaching Model

Chapter four provides an in-depth exploration of the creation of the W-O-M-A-N coaching model, emphasising its focus on gender-sensitive and women-centred coaching. The chapter opens with a personal narrative about the challenges and insights encountered during the development of the model, illustrating the importance of coaches developing their own tailored coaching methodology.

It includes "Dear Coach" letters that highlight the transformative impact of coaching on women, giving them a platform to share their experiences and validate the model's effectiveness. These letters serve as powerful testimonials, reflecting real-life applications and outcomes of the W-O-M-A-N coaching process.

Additionally, the chapter offers practical guideposts for each phase of the model: Watershed, Ownership, Milestones, Action, and New Beginnings. These guideposts are designed to assist coaches in navigating each phase effectively, providing clear, actionable steps to ensure they achieve the highest impact in their practice. The guideposts also emphasise the integration of gendered perspectives, ensuring that coaching approaches are effective and deeply relevant to the unique challenges women face.

**Chapter Five:** Mapping the Gender-Intelligent Coaching Framework

Chapter five summarises the eclectic theoretical underpinnings supporting the gender-intelligent coaching framework, showcasing how these theories shape the gendered coaching intervention. This chapter underscores the critical importance of integrating a diverse array of theoretical foundations into the gender-intelligent coaching framework. By incorporating gender theory, integral coaching, ontological coaching, integral theory, social psychology, motivational and goal attainment theories, and neuroscience, the framework offers a robust and adaptable coaching methodology. These interconnected theories not only enhance coaching interventions but also provide a comprehensive lens to examine and address a wide range of issues, particularly those related to gender dynamics. This integration supports clients in navigating societal expectations and biases, fostering a gender-equitable environment for personal and professional growth.

**Chapter Six:** Coaching Tools

Chapter six discusses the role of coaching tools in the coaching process. These tools help coaches and clients track progress, set goals, improve self-awareness, and discover new perspectives. Some of the coaching tools described are intake and post-assessment forms, the Wheel of Life, goal-setting workbooks, time-tracking worksheets, reflective diary entries, incisive and generative questioning, reframing exercises, and strength-based and personality evaluations. The chapter also discusses the GROW coaching model's application as a goal-setting tool in the gender-intelligent coaching approach.

**Conclusion:** Forward and Beyond – Embracing the Future of Gender-Intelligent Coaching

The "Forward and Beyond" chapter reflects on the journey of developing a gender-intelligent coaching approach, stressing that even though the book comes to an end, the conversation about how the coaching profession can optimally serve women coaching clients continues.

The chapter reiterates the book's theme: coaching serves as an empowering human development modality, liberating individuals from internal and external constraints. It underscores that for women, these constraints are often deeply rooted in patriarchy, misogyny, and sexism. To genuinely support women, coaches must acknowledge these barriers and transition from gender-blind coaching to a gender-intelligent coaching approach.

It also restates the book's main thesis by proposing that gender-intelligent coaching can illuminate the path for women who build their success on unwavering determination, capability, motivation, and resilience. The conclusion goes beyond coaching by urging coaches to dedicate themselves to women's empowerment, gender equity, and equality. It advocates for coaches to liberate themselves and their clients from the confines of patriarchy and pave the way for a more inclusive and thriving world.

## CHAPTER 1

# A FESTIVAL OF METAPHORS - A LITANY OF DISCRIMINATION

*"Culture does not make people. People make culture. So, if it is in fact true that the full humanity of women is not our culture, we must make it our culture."*

Chimamanda Ngozi Adichie,
(Acclaimed Author and Advocate for Gender and Social Justice)

Let's start this chapter with an imagination exercise.

Picture a pilot, a cardiac specialist, and a president.

Next, picture a philosopher, a personal development guru, and a famous coach.

Done?

Hold the images of these individuals in your memory for a moment.

Now solve a quick riddle: a father and son are in a horrible car crash that kills the dad. The son is rushed to the hospital; and just as he's about to go into surgery, the surgeon says, "I can't operate. That boy is my son!"[9] How is this possible?

Did your mental gallery of these figures lean predominantly toward males, mainly white males? Similarly, did the riddle leave you stumped for a few seconds before realising the surgeon was the boy's mother? Don't fret. You are merely joining the millions of people who, consciously or unconsciously, conform to the prevailing paradigm—or what is colloquially termed the "think leader - think male[10]" phenomenon.

## The Power of Bias

This phenomenon links authority, influence, and expertise to men, particularly white men, who have traditionally held positions of power. This association between men and authority stems from their unfettered access to power and decision-making structures rather than their exceptional aptitude. This historical advantage often reproduces the pervasive patriarchal discourse about men's innate ability for these roles, re-entrenching their privilege. One only has to point to the dearth of women representation in governance structures in the political and socio-economic landscape to understand to what extent these patriarchal views still endure today.

These ingrained biases include racism and sexism. The interrelated phenomena of racism and sexism combine to generate a powerful rhetoric capable of creating exclusionary societal structures, maintaining inequities, and denying or limiting chances for designated marginalised individuals. These biases have far-reaching consequences, perpetuating cycles of oppression and exclusion for specific groups, in particular women and people of colour.

They not only impact individuals on a personal level but also influence larger structures and institutions, reinforcing power dynamics that benefit some while marginalising others. Addressing and dismantling these biases is crucial for creating a more just and equitable society for all individuals, regardless of race, sex, gender, or other identities.

## Adaptive Consciousness: The Unseen Influences

As coaches, we require a profound understanding of the intricate web of both conscious and unconscious racism and sexism. It's like acknowledging the presence of crocodiles in the river when coaching clients. Just like in the metaphorical river, where unseen dangers lurk beneath the surface, the effects of racism and sexism can be pervasive yet often unnoticed. Our cognitive processes, or what Malcolm Gladwell calls "adaptive consciousness", greatly influence our perceptions and judgements[11]. Adaptive consciousness serves us well as the brain can quickly process information, often subconsciously, to make rapid decisions. However, while adaptive consciousness is efficient, its operation exists mainly outside our conscious awareness, which then renders it prone to being influenced by stereotypes and prejudices we consciously or unintentionally believe about other people.

## The Coach's Dilemma - Navigating Biases

This poses a pivotal question for coaches: how can we not only address the racism and sexism our clients encounter but also confront our adaptive consciousness and our own internalised forms of racism and sexism? In other words, the society we grow up in affects our thoughts, attitudes and reflexive responses, so coaches themselves are susceptible to the pervasive, deeply entrenched patriarchy and race and gender biases. After all, these patriarchal and racial ideologies have deeply permeated our collective consciousness for aeons.

So, how should coaches navigate this minefield? How do we handle the realisation that various conscious or unconscious biases inevitably shape our thoughts and actions? What does it mean for client engagement? Do we choose to conscientiously work at overcoming biases that, for instance, automatically assume specific roles, emotions, and attitudes are more suited for, or inherent to men or women? Should we stubbornly persist in our current coaching approaches, or should we courageously embark on a transformative path?

Let's complicate the challenge even more by adding another layer to the intricacies of coaching women. We humans are not simply single-dimensional beings but carry multi-identities. We embody a complex tapestry of intersecting identities. For instance, an individual who identifies as white in terms of race may also identify as a woman in terms of sexual identity, as South African in terms of nationality, and as Jewish in terms of religion. These intersecting identities create a rich mosaic that can evoke a diverse spectrum of perceptions and preconceptions in others, influencing judgements about and responses to an individual's abilities and limitations. Understanding and successfully manoeuvring through these subtleties is more than just a theoretical concept; it is a critical necessity for coaches. Who exactly are we coaching, and what challenges are they presenting? It is vital for coaches to grasp the complex nature of identity and the various societal lenses through which people are seen. A different coaching approach might be called upon depending on whether it is a black woman who is confronting systems of discrimination and shut doors or whether the woman comes from a privileged group, thus qualifying for a freer pass.

In my experience as a coach and gender specialist, effective coaching for women requires embracing an intersectional and gendered perspective. This approach recognises the various roles and unique gender-related obstacles they must surmount. It is essential that we coach the whole woman, considering the system she operates in, rather than focusing just on the coaching topics we are comfortable with!

# Intersectionality and Coaching

To illustrate further, let's examine the experience of Sara, a black Muslim woman who wears a hijab (a scarf that covers her hair). Her resume showcases her years of leadership experience and extensive qualifications. She has completed a Master's Degree in Leadership Coaching at a prestigious university and has applied for the position of CEO at, let's call it, The Coaching Association of Africa. Now, imagine that the recruitment panel consists predominantly of white men. Here's how intersectionality, which occurs when gender and race bias converge, may negatively impact Sara's chances of being appointed:

1. *Racism:* Sara may experience racism because she is black. She might also be impacted by systemic biases, which disproportionately affect black women[12]. During her interview, she might encounter racial bias, where there is a conscious or unconscious preference for men, especially white men, to hold positions of power.

2. *Ethnicity:* Sara could also experience Islamophobia due to her religious identity[13]. She might face stereotypes, prejudice, hostility, and fear based on misconceptions about her faith, her dress code, and the negative association of her faith with fundamentalism and terrorism. Stereotypes may also portray her as oppressed or submissive, rendering her unsuitable for leadership roles.

3. *Sexism:* Because she is a woman, she might encounter sexism. She could encounter gender stereotypes, such as the notion that men are more suited for leadership[14].

4. *Intersecting biases:* Sara could face simultaneous and sometimes contradictory biases—she is oppressed or submissive because of her faith, aggressive due to her race, and less capable because of her sex.

In sum, Sara carries an additional burden: not only must she present her brilliant self to the recruitment panel, but she must also navigate potential biases, prejudices, and stereotypes.

Now, imagine that immediately after Sara's interview, Steve is interviewed. Steve is a white male with similar work experience and qualifications as Sara. There are no rewards for guessing who will be more relatable to the panel. The brain is a tricky organ — for instance, when we see a person who shares our skin colour, speaks like us, and belongs to the same social groups as us, we are more likely to show more affinity towards that individual. In this instance, if the panel members are predominantly white, they may unconsciously, or perhaps consciously, favour Steve. Thus, Steve only has to prove to the interview panel he can do the job. He does not have to contend with the potholes of bias, prejudice and stereotypes that Sara had to navigate during her interview. Who do you think will secure the job appointment? Research suggests that Steven would more likely be appointed to the CEO position.

What can we do differently to mitigate these biases in the recruitment process? The ideal approach would involve conducting "blind" recruitment interviews, where the interview panel screens candidates without knowing their gender and race. While this is often not a feasible option, it has been successfully implemented in practice.

In a fascinating study aimed at changing the male-dominant composition of symphony orchestras, the orchestras implemented "blind" auditions. A screen was utilised to conceal the candidate's identity during the hiring process. This increased women's representation as symphony members from 6 percent in 1970 to 21 percent in 1993[15]. Since it is near impossible to hide the gender and race of individuals during an interviewing process, the alternative should be that the recruitment panel undergoes anti-racism and anti-sexism and diversity training. More importantly, if the interview panel were diverse, it would contribute to levelling the playing field for all the candidates by mitigating unconscious biases that may exist in choosing the "best" candidate.

While structural changes such as diverse interview panels and bias training can be used in mitigating discrimination, the reality remains that individuals like Sara still face significant challenges.

## On Being the Ideal Coach

As a coach, I have a question for you. What would happen if Sara sought coaching from you? Sara's present coaching issue is that she applied for the CEO post but was not hired. Nevertheless, during her interview, she perceived the panel's behaviour as disrespectful and suspected that she may have experienced instances of racism and sexism. Additionally, she sensed that something was off due to their biased comments. Despite this, she persevered during the interview, aiming to ensure that the interviewing panel maintained a favourable perception of her. However, after the interview, she felt it was a soul-fracturing experience and sought coaching to assist her in navigating the covert and overt bias she encountered during her interview. She also felt shame that she did not confront the panel immediately and that her instinct was to maintain composure and "professionalism" and maintain a "nice girl" demeanour.

## Are you the Ideal Coach for Her?

What I mean by an "ideal coach" is not related to the coach's race or gender. I am inquiring about your level of preparedness and expertise as a coach to effectively support a client who has experienced several instances of discrimination. As a coach, have you fully immersed yourself in diversity, inclusion, and equality discourse practices? Do you know that experiencing bias is a multifaceted ordeal and causes trauma, often accompanied by a whirlwind of emotions—anger, frustration, helplessness, fear of repercussions, and perhaps most insidiously, shame?

Are you capable of coaching a client if you have never experienced or grasped the perspective of individuals who have been targeted for discrimination? Are you aware of your own conscious and unconscious biases towards people, or, even more alarming, are you in denial of the impact of racism and sexism on human development?

The primary assertion of this book is that the coaching fraternity's raison d'être is to advance, promote, and empower people in their pursuit of excellence in both their personal and professional lives. Given the research findings on racism and sexism, it is logical to include them as variables that may prevent our coaching clients from reaching their full potential. Therefore, it makes sense for the coaching fraternity to shine a spotlight on the pressing issues of racism and sexism[16]. It will take courage for coaches to delve into the meta-question of coaching in the context of clients experiencing prejudice and discrimination. By doing this, we could clarify how discrimination affects people's personal and professional trajectories and develop coaching interventions that enable our clients to counter these biases and lessen the damaging effects of discrimination.

## The Whack-a-Mole Phenomenon

As we delve further into the complexities of biases and their impact, it becomes essential to explore how they impact women specifically. Now, I could have written pages and pages on the gendered challenges women encounter; however, I indicated from the onset this book, "*What Women Want Coaches to Know: A Gender-Intelligent Coaching Approach*", is not about lamenting sexism, gender bias, and gender stereotypes. Instead, this book will use established research to demonstrate how women continue to struggle in a world marked by sexism and bias—much like the crocodiles in the river will not disappear by just knowing they exist. In the spirit of transparency, and since this book is not a suspense novel, I will be upfront about the results of my research: patriarchy is tenacious! And the consequences can be devastating. A stark illustration of this is found in the alarming rates of violence against women, which creates a perilous environment for women.

In fact, patriarchy is said to be so tenacious it exhibits a relentless whack-a-mole tendency, liken to the popular fairground game in which, after striking one mole down, another promptly emerges[17]. This comparison mirrors the continuous cycle in which a new myth swiftly arises as we debunk one myth about women's abilities, talents, and potential.

# The 3C Women's Work Domain

When we turn our focus to the relationship between work and gender, historical viewpoints unveil a narrative portraying men as the predominant figures in public work and leadership positions. Conversely, women were pigeonholed to work in the private (domestic) sphere, relegated to roles primarily associated with caregiving, cleaning, and cooking—the so-called 3C work domain. This delineation was symptomatic of first-generation gender-based bias, which manifested in deliberate efforts to exclude women from leadership roles[18]. Such exclusion was driven by the belief that women were intellectually and emotionally inferior, perpetuating a systemic prejudice against their advancement.

Furthermore, when women were permitted in the public workspace, their positions were predominantly confined to culturally feminine caring and service work, such as secretaries, social workers, nurses, and teachers. But even in these caring-based fields, men are more likely to be advantaged over women colleagues.[19]

Thankfully, the women and feminist movement plays a crucial role in debunking the entrenched myth of "think man, think leader." Women, albeit at a snail's pace, are making their way into leadership echelons. Despite the increased representation of women in leadership positions, prevalent myths and fantasies still prevail, including:

1. ***Divine Will:*** Some societies explain women's exclusion from public and leadership roles by interpreting religious dictums as denying women their agency and deeming them inferior to men.

2. ***Biological and Emotional Dispositions:*** Many believe women are naturally nurturing and emotional. Thus, they are unsuitable for tasks that require complex decision-making and strategic thinking because they cannot handle the stress and pressure of leadership roles.

3. ***Traditional Gender Roles:*** Women are often expected to prioritise their roles as wives, mothers, and their domestic responsibilities. These roles are considered incompatible with leadership positions.

4. ***Social and Cultural Conventions:*** Social conventions and cultural expectations sometimes exclude women from leadership posts, perpetuating the belief that men are natural leaders.

It might be tempting to dismiss the above as mere beliefs, but at times, science was and can be misused to drive and support discriminatory narratives about women. Yes, the patriarchal machine is formidable and capable of biological tropes (as was the racist machinery), and dismantling its edifice demands a cohesive strategy that leaves no fissures for patriarchy to seep through.

## Gender Equality at a Snail's Pace

To prove my point and disabuse you of the idea that all of the above facts are a mere figment of my imagination, look no further than the persistent under-representation of women in leadership roles. According to recent studies in 2022, only 26,5% of women occupied positions in parliament globally, [20] and only 26% occupied CEO and senior management positions[21]. The speed of women gaining equitable representation in decision-making structures is glacial. An analogy commonly used to illustrate this incredibly slow

10

progress is that "A snail could crawl the entire length of the Great Wall of China in 212 years, just slightly longer than the 200 years it will take for women to be equally represented in Parliament[22]". This comparison vividly portrays the sluggish rate at which progress toward gender equality in political representation is made.

## Factors Contributing to Underrepresentation

The reasons for this underrepresentation of women in leadership positions, not only on the political front but also in other sectors, are not rocket science! The significant factors contributing to women's underrepresentation in leadership are:

- *Descriptive* gender stereotypes dictate what characteristics women should possess and define what "normal" behaviour is for each gender. For instance, a common stereotype might be that women are more nurturing and emotional, and men are less emotional and more assertive or logical[23].

- *Prescriptive* gender stereotypes dictate how women and men are "supposed" to act in society. For example, a prescriptive stereotype might dictate that men should be strong and independent and not show vulnerability, while women should be caring and focused on their appearance[24].

These descriptive and prescriptive gender stereotypes have enormous implications for women since they manifest in a variety of ways, including conscious and unconscious bias in hiring and firing, career development, career trajectory, career choice, stereotypes about women's leadership abilities, and so forth. And then, of course, what befuddles this debate more is some dodgy research that confirms these descriptive and prescriptive gender stereotypes and, more importantly, co-opts women to believe these stereotypes. For instance, numerous studies have disproved the notion of brain differences between men and women. Do you still remember the hype generated by the release of the book,

"Men Are from Mars, Women from Venus"?[25] It became widely popular since it confirmed the notion that men and women are fundamentally different, not just biologically, but also in terms of their communication styles, emotional needs, and relationship dynamics. The world said, "Aha, you see, men and women are different," since the book reinforced descriptive and prescriptive stereotypes. The reality is, of course, another story. What are often observed disparities between men and women are not natural or inherent. Instead, societal expectations, cultural norms, and upbringing significantly shape the perceived differences between genders. The book ignored the fact that gender is often a social construct, meaning that roles, behaviours, and expectations associated with being male or female are learned and reinforced through socialisation rather than being biologically predetermined.

The continued gender bias also means here has been a minimal shift in women's domestic workload despite their substantial increase in workforce participation[26]. Women find themselves participating at work along with being chiefly responsible for caring, cleaning and cooking[27]. There is also a continued backlash against women and men stepping outside of these gender confines[28]. This is compounded by systemic barriers such as the gender pay gap, lack of access to networking and mentorship opportunities, and limited support for professional-private life balance and organisational structures suited for men.

Societal gender expectations, often reinforced by mainstream media, wield significant influence in shaping our perceptions. It comes as no surprise that numerous studies consistently underscore the profound impact of sexist jokes, advertisements, and remarks on women's identities, reinforcing stereotypical views. Furthermore, these media influences exert considerable sway in guiding individuals towards opportunities consistent with societal and cultural norms. An intriguing study examined the impact of media exposure on girls aged between 6 and 9 years, measuring the consequences of different types of commercials on these girls' career aspirations. The findings unveiled a significant correlation: girls exposed to stereotypical career portrayals tended to lean towards traditional roles, whereas those exposed to counter-stereotypical representations exhibited a preference for non-traditional paths[29].

## A Litany of Metaphors Illuminating Gender Challenges

In our quest to understand the gendered obstacles women face in the workplace, metaphors serve as powerful tools. Much like a well-told story, a metaphor can illuminate the complexities of an issue in ways raw data cannot. These vivid comparisons capture the essence of women's experiences, articulating the often unspoken and intricate patterns of discrimination and bias they navigate daily. I found myself drawn towards the metaphors option to express women's challenges because, in the field of coaching, we harness the power of metaphors as a potent coaching tool. Why? Metaphors possess the unique ability to distil complex experiences, express the unspoken, illuminate intricate concepts and patterns, and convey the depth of experiences, emotions, and feelings. As such, I will now spotlight some of the metaphors that capture the gendered challenges women encounter in their professional journeys:

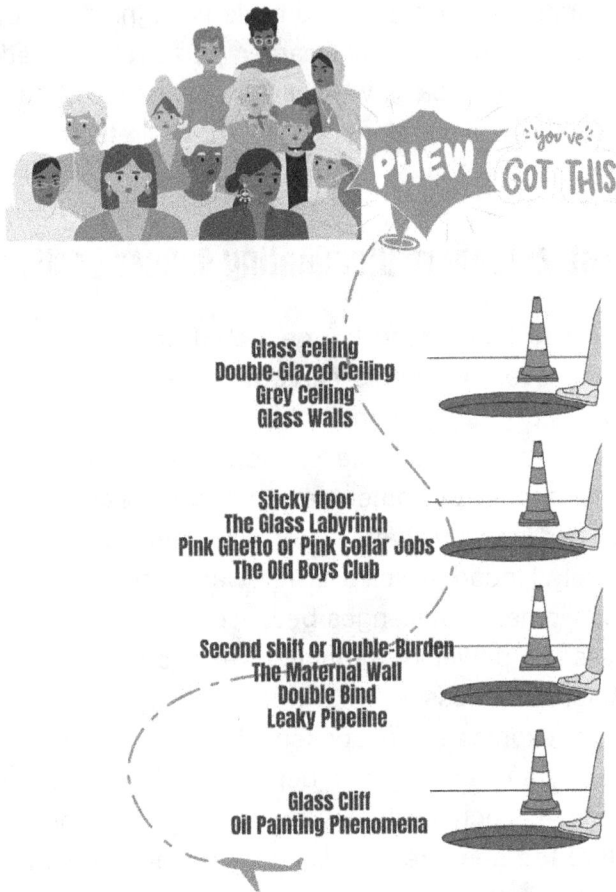

*Figure 1: Metaphors of challenges women face*

- *Glass Ceiling:* The glass ceiling metaphor vividly illustrates the invisible barrier that prevents women and minorities from advancing to higher levels of leadership. This barrier suggests that while women can see the next level in their leadership trajectory, they are unable to break through due to deep-seated gender stereotypes and discriminatory practices[30].

- *Double-glazed Glass Ceiling:* The double-glazed ceiling metaphor highlights the additional barriers, such as racial and gender prejudice, that women of colour experience due to intersecting forms of discrimination[31].

- *The Gray Ceiling or Gray Wall:* The gray ceiling and gray wall metaphors primarily address age-related discrimination. Older women are generally perceived as less talented or less valued. Whereas older men are seen as wise and experienced, older women face various penalties, including fewer prospects for promotion, limited access to training and development, and the risk of termination or even forced retirement based on age[32].

- *Glass Walls:* The glass wall metaphor captures the gender bias phenomenon that even when women gain a foothold in high management positions, they are often restricted to the role of support functions such as human resources or less strategic positions and find it challenging to advance to top executive positions[33].

- *Sticky Floor:* The sticky floor metaphor poignantly refers to the systemic barriers that trap women in low-paying, low-status jobs with minimal job security and limited opportunities for moving up the career ladder[34].

- *The Labyrinth:* The labyrinth metaphor is a fitting image to describe the unique challenges women face when navigating the complex and often opaque pathways to leadership. While men mostly find it easy to climb the proverbial leadership ladder, the "leadership labyrinth" acknowledges that women often face unexpected obstacles, twists and turns, and dead ends that are very much like an actual labyrinth[35].

- *Pink Collar Ghetto or Pink-Collar Jobs:* The pink ghetto or pink-collar metaphor refers to the concentration of women in certain jobs and industries traditionally dominated by women.

These jobs are often lower-paid, devalued, and considered lower-status jobs[36].

- *The Old Boys Club:* The "old boys club" metaphor refers to exclusive groups of powerful, privileged, and authoritative men who employ their connections to maintain influence in sectors such as corporate boardrooms, politics, social groups, professional networks, and sports. These men often capitalise on the camaraderie in their networks to enhance their professional worth and social capital. In addition, no measures are undertaken to promote diversity and inclusivity within their exclusive groups[37].

- *Second Shift or Double-Burden*: The second shift or double-burden metaphor indicates that in addition to women's paid work, they often have a significant additional unpaid work shift. The expectation to fulfil most of the household and caregiving tasks results in women having significantly larger workloads than their partners[38].

- *The Maternal Wall:* The maternal wall, also known as the motherhood penalty, vividly illustrates the discrimination working mothers face in the workplace. They are often assumed to be less committed or competent due to their caregiving responsibilities. Moreover, the necessary time off for maternity leave and parenting detrimentally impacts on women's career trajectories and salaries[39].

- *Double-Bind:* The double-bind metaphor conveys the dilemma women face when trying to conform to the conflicting expectations of gendered behaviour at work. This refers to the stereotypical myths that women should be warm, collaborative and caring leaders or present as "take care" leaders. In contrast, men are expected to be "take-charge" leaders because they are agentic, assertive and decisive. The double-bind women leaders face is that when they do display "take care" leadership styles, they are negatively judged as ineffective leaders, yet, when they adopt a "take-charge" leadership style, they are also negatively judged as being too "male-like"[40].

- *Leaky Pipeline:* The leaky pipeline describes the phenomenon of women exiting the workforce at different career stages due to discriminatory practices, lack of support and the challenge of balancing work-life demands[41].

- *Glass Cliff:* The glass cliff metaphor captures the occurrence of women being assigned to positions of authority during times of organisational crisis or difficulties, where there is a significant probability of failure to redirect the organisation. The women are then blamed for the failure, reinforcing the self-fulfilling prophecy of women not being leadership-worthy [42].

- *Oil Painting Phenomenon*: The oil painting phenomenon, a term I coined, describes the practice of showcasing a few women or a few black people at the leadership level to create an illusion of diversity. However, without genuine transformation programs to address inclusion, diversity, and transformation, the organisation remains a cauldron of racism and sexism, despite appearing bias-free from the outside.

As I write this, additional metaphors spring to mind, since the evolving nature of biases and discrimination against women ceases to stop. I hope by grasping these few metaphors, and the challenges women have to deal with, you've come to value the importance of advocating for developing a gender-intelligent coaching approach – one that incorporates understanding gender dynamics, gender biases, and discrimination.

While gender-intelligent coaching can serve as a coaching approach for both men and women, this book focuses explicitly on its application for women as they shoulder the impact of sexism, gender bias, and gender stereotyping.

For these reasons, one of the book's central theses is that coaches must understand and acknowledge the gendered landmines women encounter when coaching them. I must also emphasise that the term "coach" is used in this book to refer to all coaches, both men and women. It is crucial for both female and male coaches to comprehend the specific barriers and biases women face to provide truly effective coaching.

Let me clarify the language issue. Often, the terms "women" and "gender" are conflated. When we hear the term "gender," we assume it refers solely to women. However, gender refers to the socially constructed roles, behaviours, and attributes that a given society consider appropriate for men and women based on their assigned sex at birth—being born female or male. Recognising this distinction allows us to address the unique challenges women and men face when society forces them to conform to societal expectations. Thus, gender norms pigeonhole both men and women. For instance, gender norms dictate that men should be strong and stoic while women should be nurturing and emotional. These gender expectations of men to suppress their emotions, as well as the perception of women's expression of emotions as a sign of weakness, have a negative impact on both men and women. This dynamic impacts everyone, illustrating the pervasive nature of gender bias and by understanding these gender dynamics, we can better appreciate the complex web of expectations and stereotypes that shape our lives.

## Toward a Gender-Intelligent Coaching Approach

"Now, why is this book only focusing on women?" you might ask. Well, the answer is obvious: It is women who predominantly encounter gendered challenges. So, it makes sense to begin the discussion with a book on coaching women to deal with the gender-challenging environments they encounter. However, this emphasis does not preclude implementing a gender-intelligent coaching approach to coach men to ensure they, too, are not blind to how the gender discourse impacts them.

Therefore, 'What Women Want Coaches to Know' centres on and addresses the unique obstacles and opportunities women face in a gendered society. By focussing on women initially, it creates the impetus for expanding the discussion on diversity, inclusion and equality.

Notably, within the dynamic realm of coaching, coaches act as mirrors, reflecting not just the visible aspects but also illuminating concealed blind spots. This reflective role is crucial in uncovering the often-overlooked gendered challenges women face in their professional and personal lives.

By adopting a gender-intelligent coaching approach, we not only acknowledge the existence of these gendered challenges that confront our women clients, but we also endeavour to understand the significant impact on our clients' professional and personal lives and how this may impede their progress. By bringing these issues to light, we equip our clients with the tools and insights they need to navigate these complexities with confidence and resilience. Furthermore, we also contribute to addressing systemic barriers and fostering a more diverse and inclusive workplace culture for both men and women.

It also intends to shine a light on how gender-intelligent coaching aims to create an inclusive and supportive environment where women clients can explore and navigate their goals and aspirations in a way that respects and addresses their gender-related needs and concerns. This approach may involve tailored strategies and interventions that consider the complexities of gender dynamics, ultimately fostering greater awareness, empowerment, and growth for our women clients.

Certainly, I expect some pushback to the proposition that coaches must wear gender lenses when coaching. However, my response was and still is that we use our business lenses when we coach business people, our entrepreneurial lenses when we coach entrepreneurs, and so forth. Hence, the gender-intelligent coaching approach requests wearing your gender lenses as your superpower as a coach since we know we live in a gendered world.

I have, on many occasions, engaged various coaches about whether they are coaching on the gender-specific or race challenges women encounter. Often their retort is, "My female clients have never presented race and gender issues as coaching concerns!" This might be the truth. However, if our coaching does not focus on asking insightful questions about race or gender, our clients will unlikely raise these issues themselves. Consider this: research indicates that 51% of women of colour experience racism at work[43]. But in your coaching practice you are telling me when you coach women of colour, the topic of racism does not present as a coaching issue. How is this discrepancy possible?

The reason for the silence on racism or sexism might be because our female coaching clients lack the vocabulary to articulate their experience of gender bias and racism or feel these are not suitable coachable topics. Another reason, why it might not show up as a coaching issue, and which I alluded to earlier in this chapter, is that patriarchy and its manifestation are tenacious and don't just flip over and die at the first sign of opposition; instead, it merely adapts and resurfaces in new guises. This phenomenon resembles the mythological Hydra: cut off one head, and two more grow in its place. In contemporary discourse, these resurgences manifest as what scholars term "second-generation bias" or "modern sexism"[44].

Second-generation bias is a particularly insidious form of prejudice that operates covertly, lurking beneath the surface of seemingly egalitarian workplaces. Unlike hostile sexism, where there is outright opposition to gender equality, it cloaks itself in subtlety, conforming to the prevailing norms and regulations of the modern corporate landscape. However, it frequently manifests as benevolent sexism, where men treat women kindly because they perceive them as weak and dependent on their protection and support[45]. This stealthy nature makes it even more challenging to identify and address.

Envisioning second-generation bias as the roots growing under the surface of a seemingly tranquil garden can be helpful. Though hidden, these roots exert a powerful influence, shaping the landscape above ground. Similarly, second-generation bias, deeply ingrained in our cultural consciousness, continues to influence our actions. These biases tend to operate subconsciously, influencing our perceptions and behaviours without our explicit awareness. Unfortunately, they seep into the collective psyche of society and uphold long-held assumptions about gender roles. Despite attempts to eradicate the root causes of bias, they lurk under the surface, in the shadows, and continue to wield their influence.

Second-generation bias manifests itself in a variety of ways, including implicit bias, microaggression, and the continuation of gender stereotypes.

Research identifies several examples of how second-generation bias continue to impact women's progress in the workplace:

- He-peating: People dismiss or ignore a woman's recommendation, even if it's worthy. Conversely, when a male colleague makes the same recommendation, it receives recognition and appreciation. This behaviour, known as "he-peating" or "mansplaining," occurs when men replicate the ideas of women and take credit for them[46].

- He-tribution: Despite performing the same tasks as men, women often receive less credit for their labour. This may be due to self-attribution bias, which arises because men tend to be more assertive in claiming their accomplishments and taking credit for their efforts. In contrast, women are more likely to downplay their accomplishments and attribute credit to others[47].

- Relatedness: Men often have access to opportunities that women do not, such as invitations to male-only socialising events like golf or after-work socials, thereby excluding women from opportunities for professional networking or, conversely, developing relatedness. This marginalisation makes it difficult for women to cultivate relatable connections and advance professionally, perpetuating a cycle of marginalisation[48].

- Penalty for caregiving: Women face more significant discrimination than men when they take time off work to care for their children or elderly parents. Upon their return, the repercussions await them such as being overlooked for promotion since their absence in the office is regarded as an indicator of lack of commitment. Again, in this instance, the backlash is against the working woman, not against the operating male-centric organisational system[49].

- The enduring pay gap: Even though it may be against the law to pay women less than men for the same work, it is not uncommon for women to earn less. This enduring pay gap manifests itself through the distribution of bonuses, biased performance evaluations, placement in lower-paying professions or sectors, and the underrepresentation of women in leadership roles and women starting at a lower salary[50].

- It is raining men: Many organisational systems remain geared towards a predominantly male workforce, with little regard for the diverse professional and private responsibilities of women. For example, an organisational culture that rewards long hours and office presence, lack on-site childcare facilities, lack flexible work arrangements or flexible hours, reinforces a male-centric work environment.[51]

Although second-generation bias may not be as apparent as its predecessor, outright sexism or first-generation gender bias, it significantly impedes women's opportunities for progress and success. This chapter delved into the intricate and complex gender challenges women encounter and bravely navigate, particularly when they ascend to leadership positions. We uncovered the substantial burden of ingrained and implicit race and gender stereotypes, which disproportionately darken the path for women, particularly women of colour. This chapter also emphasised the importance of understanding the interwoven fabric of social identities, as well as how our intersectional identities impact women's private and professional lives.

The time has come for the coaching fraternity to take action and empower women with the tools and insights offered by gender-intelligent coaching. But, of course, we can only do so if we, as a profession, are ready to acknowledge that both coaches and clients live in a gendered world, therefore our coaching offerings cannot be gender-blind. The well-being and success of our clients, especially women, depend on our ability to embrace the nuances of gendered experiences in our coaching practices.

It's a paradigm shift in coaching that demands our unwavering commitment, compassion, and competence. Only by doing so can we hope to co-create a future where gender ceases to be a barrier, allowing all individuals, regardless of gender, to reach their full potential.

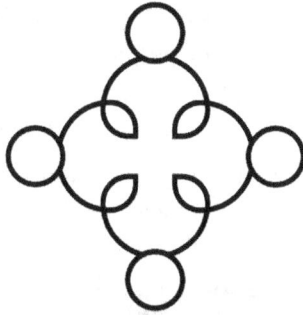

# CHAPTER 2

# COACHING FOR DIVERSITY, EQUALITY AND INCLUSION

*"It is not easy being a woman anywhere. Moreover, for women leaders, the obstacles are greater, the demands are greater and the double standards are greater."*

Benazir Bhutto
(Assassinated former Prime Minister of Pakistan)

Coaching is the buzzword right now! It has presented itself as the newly confident and sassy kid on the block in the personal development, goal attainment, and self-actualisation industries, promising to unlock new frontiers in human purpose, potential, and productivity.

In the past, the word "coach" almost exclusively conjured images of sport, such as a rugby or soccer coach. Nowadays, the term "coach" is associated with personal and professional growth, competing with more established professions like therapy, counselling, and mentoring in the public imagination. Coaching's growing traction can be attributed partly to renowned personal development gurus touting coaching as a panacea for overcoming human *stuck-ness* and a catalyst for realising one's full potential. Furthermore, successful global icons, other than sports icons, publicly credit their success to their coach's role in their lives. These coaches, in turn, have coaches, who have coaches, who have coaches. I think you get where I'm going with this. The coaching industry is a blooming and booming business!

## Defining Coaching and Who Can Coach

However, the fuss about the birth of any new profession or discipline is to be expected: all new professions are welcomed with much hoopla and fanfare. Yet, emerging professions face their own set of challenges. For coaching, the foremost challenges that confound the coaching profession are defining the essence and purpose of coaching as well as who has the authority to claim the title of "coach." Then there are the myriads of coaching methodologies that all fall under the coaching banner, adding to the difficulty of defining coaching. Furthermore, over the last decade, the profession has grappled with the fundamental question of whether coaching itself is a neutral and apolitical methodology.

Are you willing to indulge me and do a quick exercise? Access your search engine and type, "What is coaching?" When I conducted this search, it took less than 0.40 seconds to retrieve a staggering 13,360,000,000 results. In light of these results, it becomes apparent that, while there are many definitions of coaching, there is no universally accepted definition[52]. Even though the academic coaching literature has devoted considerable space to the subject, a consensus on the standard de jure definition of coaching remains elusive. Further complicating matters is that the terms *coaching*, *mentoring*, *counselling*, *therapy*, and *training* are often used interchangeably. In addition, people who pursue coaching come from diverse fields and thus adopt diverse coaching approaches, methodologies, and foci. It's undeniably evident from the literature that these critical aspects, the definition of coaching and who is qualified to provide coaching, require resolution. However, the coaching profession is caught in a catch-twenty-two situation. On the one hand, the inflow of people who identify as "coaches" given their diverse experience and expertise, brings considerable innovation to the coaching profession. On the other hand, the lack of standardisation, in terms of the breadth of coaching and the qualification of coaches, leaves the coaching profession open for role ambiguity, lack of standardisation and serious ethical considerations regarding competence, confidentiality, and clients' well-being. Importantly, and often ignored, is that given the undefined parameters of coaching methodologies, it can also be used to entrench a unipolar view of the world and adopt dominant but dodgy discourses. It is equally capable of promoting a world in which people are entirely focused on their own personal growth and chase their desired outcome above all else, and remain indifferent to the effects their actions have on society and the environment.

### *Resolving the Challenges of the Title, "Coach"*

Although coaching regulatory organisations are playing catch up to ensure that individuals using the title "coach" have at least some minimum coaching training and paperwork or are at least a member of a coaching regulatory body, at this juncture in the coaching profession trajectory, the coaching industry remains largely self-regulated and depends on coaches to monitor themselves. Despite these efforts to get coaches registered, anyone can still operate as a coach without being part of any affiliated coaching organisation or undergoing a formal credentialing process. It is hoped as the profession continues to evolve, all coaches will eventually possess some form of regulatory qualification to support their practice.

## The Niche Coaching Offerings

Another confounding issue in the coaching profession, which is not observed in other professions, is the addition of adjectives or prefixes before the noun "coach." For example, in medicine or engineering, a doctor or engineer may specialise in a field such as civil engineering or cardiology based on their academic training and qualifications. However, in the field of coaching, excluding sports coaching with its specialised focus on athletic performance, we encounter a vast array of coaching specialities. These are often distinguished by various prefixes not necessarily based on recognised requisite specialisations or recognised regulatory institutions to bestow these adjectives to the noun "coach".

The variety of coaching specialisations results from coaching practitioners pointing their focus to specific niches and disciplines, anchoring their interventions in diverse theoretical frameworks or, at times, driven by their personal experience. This proliferation of coaching niches has given rise to a plethora of prefixes, including health, financial, maternity, career, transition, business, executive, leadership, retirement, performance, couple, parental, relationship, writing, dating, grief and many more that can fill a few pages in this book. The permutations of coaching offerings seem endless, highlighting the multifaceted nature of the field and showcasing the myriad ways coaches cater to unique client needs or preferred clients.

However, alongside the proliferation of coaching niches and prefixes lies a set of challenges. These prefixes are self-determined and self-regulated. With such a broad landscape of offerings, clients may struggle to navigate and identify the most suitable coaching approach for their needs, and coaching practitioners may face difficulty establishing credibility and expertise because the terms "coach" and "coaching" have such wide interpretations.

One way in which this challenge has been addressed is to divide the coaching offerings into two dominant and overarching coaching streams: life coaching and business coaching. While life coaching focuses primarily on personal development, business coaching occurs in an organisational and work setting and encompasses organisational, staff or team, executive, and leadership coaching. Business coaching targets three main areas: the individual's performance and role within an organisation, their relationships within the workplace, and aligning the individual's performance with organisational goals. Understanding these dominant streams contextualises the broader discussion of coaching practices and their respective aims. However, regardless of life coaching or business coaching, the overarching goal of these coaching variants is to optimise personal, professional, or organisational growth and development[53].

## Defining the Coaching Parameters

To ensure its continued success, the coaching profession is resolutely moving forward to define what coaching is and what differentiates it from other human development professions. Among the myriad definitions, coaching emerges as a methodology that adheres to the following values:

1.  The relationship between the coach (the one who coaches) and the coaching client, or the "coachee" (the one receiving coaching), is non-hierarchical and characterised by equality, collaboration, and a mutual commitment to learning and transformation. The term "coachee" is contentious in the coaching community, and I, too, avoid it, opting instead for "coaching client".

2.  The coaching process is intended to be a learning, introspective, and reflective journey for both the coach and the coaching client.

3. The ultimate goal of coaching is to maximise an individual's capacity for self-actualisation and present themselves as the best version of themselves by cultivating practices, habits, and behaviours that foster self-efficacy, growth, and goal achievement.

# The Birth of Coaching

Now that we have pinned down some of the key challenges faced by the coaching profession, I think it makes sense to first test the soil of the coaching profession for its values regarding gender equality, diversity, and inclusion before making a case for a gender-intelligent coaching approach. I see the coaching industry as a garden. Just as a garden needs rich, balanced, and toxin-free soil to grow healthy plants, the coaching profession needs a supportive environment to thrive.

In this analogy, the garden represents the coaching profession, and the soil symbolises the foundational principles of diversity, inclusion, and equality. Before we can focus on cultivating specific plants—like gender-intelligent coaching or coaching for women—we need to ensure that the soil is fertile and supportive. This means the coaching industry must critically examine and enrich its own practices, ensuring they are inclusive and equitable.

So, let's start this exploration by focusing on the soil that birthed the coaching profession. Reports reveal the story of an amazingly current, flourishing industry that began as a cottage industry and has now gained worldwide prominence over the course of three decades. The growth of coaching was largely due to the disenchantment with traditional approaches to personal and professional development, which catalysed the emergence of coaching as a viable alternative[54]. In addition, the growth of coaching was initially ignited within the crucible of the business sector, where coaching arose as a potent antidote to underperformance and the promise of increased productivity and positive return on investment.

However, as the coaching community matured, it recognised the peril of perpetuating the misconception that coaching is in the business of fixing the underachievers. Recognising this challenge, coaching practitioners pursued a rebranding initiative in which they endeavoured to dispel the stigma surrounding seeking coaching, affirming that it signified a commitment to growth rather than a testament to inadequacy.

Another factor contributing to the growth of coaching was the seismic shift that reverberated through the business landscape of the 21st century. This shift challenged age-old traditional leadership paradigms and moved from conventional top-down and command-and-control management to yielding a new ethos championing collaboration, adaptability, and inspiring leadership modelling. This marked the birth of transformative and servant leadership, a philosophy emphasising the power of fostering growth and innovation through shared vision and mutual respect.

Coaching entered the scene perfectly poised to catalyse this evolution. By guiding leaders, managers, and employees, coaching catalysed personal and organisational transformation. It went beyond mere skill-building; coaching honed interpersonal skills, empowering individuals to forge stronger connections and drive engagement among colleagues and direct reports. Moreover, coaching expanded its scope to encompass entire teams and systems, recognising true transformation demands a holistic approach. As a result, the impact of coaching has been nothing short of remarkable.

The International Coaching Federation (ICF), a global regulatory body for coaching, attests to this explosive growth. According to their latest figures, the coaching industry surged to unprecedented heights, with global revenue skyrocketing to a staggering $4.564 billion in 2019—an astonishing 60% increase from just two years prior[55].

And just when it seemed coaching couldn't soar any higher, it received an unprecedented endorsement from none other than the queen of self-help and self-development, Oprah Winfrey, who featured coaching on the cover of her magazine accompanied by a promotional coaching article in that edition[56]. The Oprah-effect is legendary because when Oprah mentions an item, it is considered "O-blessed". The consequence is that it makes the mentioned product shine like a golden staff adorned with diamonds, which, consequently, sells like hot pancakes! Oprah's spotlight on coaching propelled its significance to new heights, cementing its status as a force for positive change in the world.

## Laying the Ground for the Gender-Intelligent Coaching Approach

To lay the groundwork for the implementation of a gender-intelligent coaching approach, it is essential to contextualise it within the broader trajectory of the coaching profession's evolution. Initially, I contemplated embarking on a very detailed exploration of coaching's historical roots. However, given the wealth of readily accessible information on the coaching profession's history, I opted for brevity, trusting your ability to delve into this subject independently. In any case, I was mindful of my tendency to be long-winded; thus, I heeded my editor's advice, who wisely recommended directing readers to authoritative sources rather than providing exhaustive summaries.

You may need clarification as to why reflecting on the pioneers of the coaching profession is important. The reason for the focus on the coaching pioneers is that they profoundly shaped the profession's zeitgeist. In all disciplines, and so too for coaching, the founders of a profession set the agenda and culture of a profession, and the predominant ideologies, philosophies, trends, priorities, and needs of a particular era shape the profession. These pathbreakers spearhead solutions to the issues, context, and demographics they encounter, while the methodology is informed by the prevailing worldview of the time.

## The Founding Fathers of Coaching

In the case of coaching, the founding fathers—yes, I am deliberately using this term—since reading the history of the founders of coaching, it appears the formative figures in the coaching industry were predominantly men, and evidently, the earliest book on coaching was also authored by men[57].

As an aside, the emphasis on men as the initial thought leaders in the coaching profession raises an intriguing question: Were influential women who helped shape the establishment of the coaching profession overlooked, as has often been the case in other fields? Which thought leaders have shaped and are shaping the coaching industry is a compelling inquiry that warrants further exploration, and I assume this would make for a good master's or PhD topic. The challenge has now been set. I hope you accept the challenge, and I invite you to share your findings with us.

## Diverse Minds, Diverse Coaching Literature

To assess whether members of the coaching profession have been grappling with the discourse of diversity, inclusion and equality, I employed a straightforward albeit unscientific method: analysing the gender diversity of authors contributing to its published works. This approach reveals the individuals deemed authoritative or influential within the industry.

My investigation led me to explore coaching books on Amazon—a widely recognised source for mainstream coaching literature—and KR Publishing, the preeminent publisher of coaching books in South Africa. I found on Amazon's book platform that coaching books, particularly those with academic relevance and not self-published, are still predominantly authored by men[58]. However, a more encouraging trend is emerging from KR Publishing—I was delighted to discover a better representation of women-authored coaching books, signalling a positive shift towards greater inclusivity and gender diversity within the coaching publishing sphere in South Africa[59].

In literature, the diversity of authors—across gender, race, ethnicity, nationality, and location—enriches the tapestry of perspectives and experiences available to readers. This diversity is not merely an issue of representation; it is how knowledge, thematic exploration and viewpoints are cultivated in a society and a profession. For example, a black woman coach might offer insights into race and gender that a white male coach might be unable to capture with the same authenticity. Diverse authors also broaden the intellectual discourse by introducing alternative perspectives challenging the status quo and encouraging the profession to consider alternative viewpoints. This intellectual diversity is essential for promoting innovation and progress in the coaching field.

In addition, the published works also mirror the essence of the coaching profession's zeitgeist at specific times. Therefore, by systematically reviewing the coaching literature, we can uncover how these written works reveal the prevailing preoccupations, aspirations, and challenges within our field at any given moment.

## Tributaries for Change: Addressing Diversity in Coaching

In reviewing the coaching profession literature on the theme of diversity, particularly, gender diversity and the focus on racism, the coaching opinion-makers posit that the coaching profession is slow on the uptake in dealing with issues of diversity, equality, and inclusion[60]. In particular, the coaching profession has been accused of ignoring the experience of people of colour and operating under the guise of "colour-blindness"[61].

However, failing to acknowledge within the coaching industry the specific challenges people of colour and women encounter because of their race and gender is analogous—and yes, I am going for the river and crocodile analogy again. Yet, this time, we depict the coaching industry as the main river, while the tributaries, representing individual coaches, flow into the river. If the river is to thrive and support a diverse ecosystem, it must be clean and pollution-free. If there are crocodiles, representing entrenched biases and systemic barriers, they must be managed as they pose a hazardous environment to the tributaries and the broader ecosystem.

The key to a thriving river system, and by extension, a flourishing coaching profession, lies in the diversity and vitality of its tributaries. Each tributary, representing diverse and thriving coaches, enriches the main river, leading to a more dynamic and inclusive environment.

However, thus far, the profession is cautious about discussing issues of race and gender since the dominant view is that coaching, and its modality and processes are apolitical and neutral[62]. This coaching neutrality means that developing discourses about diversity within the profession and discourses about the diverse coaching clients we serve is, therefore, not a priority.

However, the coaching profession is also faced with a critical dilemma. There has been an uptake of organisations contracting coaching interventions as a strategy to enhance diversity, particularly gender diversity within organisations[63]. The question then arises: Can the coaching industry be at the cutting edge of coaching for gender diversity if it is unwilling to engage with diversity issues within the coaching profession?

Furthermore, a critical examination is necessary. When coaches are contracted to coach for gender diversity, who do the organisations automatically assign to participate in coaching interventions to reduce gender imbalances and create gender diversity within the organisation? Based on the literature, it is evident it is not the men in the organisation who are sent for coaching to address the gender diversity challenges. Still, the tendency is to assign women in the organisation for coaching, which presupposes that women are supposed to correct the gender imbalance (read: unequal representation of women in decision-making structures)[64]. Is it entirely possible that, somehow, coaching was presented as the magic wand to overcome gender diversity by coaching women? In turn, by coaching women, is the hope that the gender diversity crisis will disappear within these organisations?

Surely, logic would suggest that if gender diversity is a challenge in an organisation, it would be pragmatic to address the root causes that produce gender imbalances in the first place. And let's be real. Placing the pressure on women to fix the problem isn't fair or effective. A plethora of compelling research findings have made it crystal clear: the lack of gender diversity and lack of women's representation in leadership positions often stem from ingrained gender stereotypes and gender biases that are baked into people and the organisational system[65]. It follows then that when addressing gender diversity through coaching interventions, there is a pivotal choice for coaches to make: should coaching solely focus on women, or does it broaden the focus to coach the women within a system or zoom out further and coach for resistance to the social context—which is defined as the overall setting in which the coaching is being offered.

Of course, the other meta question remains: Who will be contracted to do the diversity coaching? This brings us to three significant dilemmas currently confronting the coaching industry. Firstly, there's a prevailing belief that coaching – its coaches, approaches, models, and tools – is inherently neutral and devoid of ideological influence and, therefore, does not perpetuate biases and stereotype tropes. A notion I think is fundamentally flawed.

Secondly, coaching educational institutions often churn out coaches who perpetuate race and gender blindness due to the absence of race and gender discourses that form part of the curriculum and the absence of race and gender diversity training within the coaching curriculums.

Lastly, while there's a growing acknowledgement of the need to address systemic perspectives and issues of race and gender in the coaching community, this perspective has yet to gain widespread acceptance in the coaching industry since the gatekeepers in the coaching industry are still of the opinion that diversity does not matter.

My view, drawn from personal experience of working in the coaching industry and supported by coaching literature, is there is currently a significant oversight in addressing gender and race issues. In fact, there is not only a lack of attention to these critical areas but also pushback driven by fear that addressing issues of race and gender within the coaching industry might create a political wobble.

However, given the coaching profession's fundamental purpose of aiding human development, it cannot afford to be hesitant about the ubiquitous effect of patriarchy within the profession and on our coaching clients. Our professional reputation depends on encouraging brave discussions about fundamental ethical concerns, especially in the setting of our increasingly diverse, multicultural societies. Therefore, recognising the profound influence of historical and present gendered and racial systems on both our own and our clients' identities is critical. By doing so, we dispel the myth that coaching is apolitical or free of racism and sexism and has nothing to contribute to these moral discussions. Furthermore, promoting the principle of respect for our clients requires acknowledging the tremendous detrimental effects of racism and sexism on our clients' lives.

To create an inclusive and no-harm-to-people profession, the coaching profession should heed the lessons learnt, for example, from the experiences of health and mental health professionals. They were forced to undertake deep introspection into their racism and sexism due to the malevolent practices committed against black people and black women, in particular[66]. Despite this introspection, no truth and reconciliation commission was held to investigate how racism, sexism and pure ignorance were sustained in these professions.

Learning from these insights and lessons and avoiding repeating the mistakes of older professions, the coaching industry has the opportunity to incorporate race and gender discourse into its DNA and become a force for anti-racism, anti-sexism, inclusion, and diversity. Notably, gender-intelligent coaching, rather than gender-blind coaching, could serve as a critical approach to bringing about meaningful transformation.

Recognising these challenges, the coaching industry must commit to fostering an environment of true inclusivity and equity. It is what the world demands of us since the research findings are clear: we live in a world where women are discriminated against based on their biological sex, and women of colour face a double-discrimination burden—biases against their sex and race.

## The Case for Gender-Intelligent Coaching

At the beginning of this book, I promised you that my motivation in advocating for coaches to adopt a gender-intelligent coaching approach is not based on emotion but backed up with hard evidence to support the case for the implementation of gender-intelligent coaching.

## The Impact of Race Bias on Women

So, let me begin with the story of Kalisha White, a woman of colour[67]. She applied for a team leader's position at Target, an American multinational company. She was not successful in her application. However, on a hunch that something was amiss, she resubmitted an identical resumé under another name that sounded white. She wanted to test her suspicion. After submitting her white-sounding name resumé, she was gobsmacked to be short-listed for an interview. She sued Target and won a class-action lawsuit.

If you think that she is the exception, numerous studies have found that this is the ugly way of the world in which women and people of colour operate. In one research study, economists from Berkeley and Chicago University submitted 83,000 job applications to 108 Fortune 500 companies, half with white-sounding names and half with black-sounding names. Despite having credentials similar to white applicants, black applicants were called back 10% fewer times across the board and even less when it came to specific companies[68].

## The Impact of Gender Bias on Women

Several studies have also been conducted to point out that even before women's abilities are tested, they are already at a disadvantage since gender bias starts in the recruitment process. For instance, one study tested for gender bias by sending out identical fictitious resumes with the same qualifications but the sole difference being the sex of the applicants' names[69]. The finding showed employers were more likely to choose male candidates than equally competent women, implying a clear gender bias against women. Interestingly, the study revealed that bias decreased when women had higher qualifications but increased when women were mothers.

Numerous studies also reveal a disconcerting impact gender bias and gender discrimination have on working women. For instance, when women leaders display assertive behaviour similar to their equally successful male peers, women are often penalised by being perceived as less likeable. I thought this cartoon (Figure 2) captures the very essence of how a similar attribute can be evaluated differently based on the individual's sex and the gender prescripts we have assigned to men and women[70].

*Figure 2: What's the difference between being assertive and aggressive?*

Since coaching speaks the language of empowerment, development, potential and so forth, there is the expectation that the coaching sector will align with practices that promote equality. In other words, will we instinctively be "walking our talk"? The coaching discipline's genesis stems from its singular goal of being a profession where *human advancement and progress* are the central focus. Hence, it should be a necessary corollary that our coaching interventions, due to our inherent task of advancing people for success, ought *not* to be a "one strategy fits all" approach.

## Addressing Patriarchy in Coaching

Furthermore, patriarchy is also crafty and tenacious, insidiously ingraining itself into the very fabric of society. It conceals itself under the garb of normality, making it all too easy for us to get trapped in its web without realising it. When it comes to the coaching profession, it's critical to understand that patriarchy is more than just an abstract idea; it's a pervasive force that influences every part of our lives, including the way we coach and are being coached.

For instance, within the coaching realm, it is not surprising that I recently saw an advert on Facebook inviting women to attend a coaching session to become better wives—yes, to be super empowered to be at the "beck and call of one's husband".

We must, therefore, accept that the coaching profession is immune to patriarchal influences. Moreover, it is not enough to acknowledge the presence of patriarchy, sexism, and racism; we must also understand we have not been immunised against it, and so we should actively try to eradicate them within our practices and in the larger coaching community.

In sum, we should start acknowledging that when we coach women and refuse to consider the pressures and challenges they face due to gender bias and stereotypes, it's like asking a swimmer to dive into a river without warning her that it's crocodile-infested. Ignoring these critical factors not only undermines the coaching process but also puts women at a severe disadvantage.

Furthermore, merely knowing about patriarchy does not suffice to protect women from its impact. Often, we mistakenly believe empowering women, in essence, adopting the "fix-the-women" perspective, will enable them to reach their full potential[71]. However, coaching should not ignore the crocodile-infested river, naively assuming the swimmer's courage alone will offer ample defence against crocodiles. This approach neglects the systemic issues that create barriers for women in the first place.

Patriarchal systems have repeatedly shown us that such a system makes it increasingly difficult for women to live full lives, let alone succeed. Furthermore, it places unfair and unwarranted pressure on women to achieve unrealistic expectations and goals. In addition, it sets women up for failure both professionally and personally, which has a damaging and devastating impact on women's physical and mental health.

Fortunately, if we hasten to do more to overcome our gendered cognitive blindness and work towards providing customised coaching that addresses women's gendered challenges, we will be well equipped as a profession to serve women brilliantly. By acknowledging and addressing women's unique challenges, we can create a more supportive and effective coaching environment that fosters sustainable growth and success.

The primary inquiry of this book revolves around the preparedness of the coaching profession to tackle the distinct obstacles that women encounter while simultaneously balancing the promotion of individual empowerment and furthering gender equality. It motivates an effective coaching approach that ought to prioritise the cultivation of individual abilities while also promoting systemic restructuring to establish non-racist and non-sexist workplace environments.

It points out that a gender-intelligent coaching approach is not just a trend but an essential part of the evolution of the coaching profession. By embracing gender-intelligent coaching, the profession can be pivotal in driving gender equality and inclusivity. This approach will benefit individual clients and contribute to broader organisational and societal change.

It further underscores that through personalised coaching offerings, coaches can coach clients to overcome barriers and biases that may prevent them from thriving while also coaching individuals to work towards dismantling discriminatory practices within organisations and society. By addressing individual and systemic factors, coaching can drive meaningful progress towards a more equitable and inclusive society.

A coach might, for example, coach a woman manager struggling to advance in her career due to gender biases at work. The coaching can be directed to assist her in navigating these challenges while also empowering her to advocate for changes in policies and practices that perpetuate discrimination against women in the workplace.

In conclusion, gender-intelligent coaching is not just a valuable tool—it is a necessity to foster equitable and thriving societies and, specifically, workplaces. The evidence is clear: when women are supported through thoughtful, tailored coaching interventions, they excel, as do the organisations they lead and contribute to. As coaches, we have the opportunity and responsibility to champion this change, ensuring our practices reflect and promote the values of diversity, equality, and inclusion.

## CHAPTER 3

# PAINTING THE CANVAS FOR A GENDER-INTELLIGENT COACHING APPROACH

*"With every experience, you alone are painting your canvas, thought by thought, choice by choice."*

Oprah Winfrey
(Media Mogul, TV Host, Philanthropist, Author)

Oprah Winfrey is spot-on when she advocates for utilising one's life experiences to shape our unique way of being in the world. However, as we pursue a learning journey, we cannot only draw from our personal experiences, but we should also learn from the experiences of others and incorporate all these insights to navigate our lives. It makes sense, does it not? As my spouse often quips, "Falling into an unknown pothole on your life journey is an experience; falling into the same one you've seen someone else fall in is foolishness."

I took these lessons to heart: learn from my experience, lean on the experiences of others, and try not to fall into the same potholes that others have already fallen into. And if I happen to fall into an old pothole, the strategy is to get out of it as quickly as possible. Of course, it is crucial to reflect on that pothole experience, learn from it, and strive to avoid it and not make the same mistake.

In keeping with this spirit, I used my personal experience and the experiences of other coaches to paint my unique gender-intelligent coaching canvas. In doing so, I aimed to build a coaching framework that draws from others' wisdom, my coaching experience and the acknowledgement of women's experiences of contending with patriarchy.

## Coaching Values and Principles

However, before I share with you how I developed my unique gender-intelligent coaching approach, which encompasses the coaching framework, the coaching model, and coaching tools, I think it is crucial that I am upfront about my principles and values of working with people. As coaches, we cannot work with people without establishing the crucial guiding values we hold about human beings since these values manifest in our coaching approach and coaching relationships.

- Profound Respect: I am committed to consistently treating my clients with profound respect. I'm always armed with large doses of curiosity and work hard not to make assumptions about my clients. Furthermore, I endeavour to employ the most suitable coaching methodologies to assist my clients in self-actualising and showing up in the world as their best version.

- Unique Individuality: I value and honour each person's distinctiveness by attentively listening to their individual narratives and intricate life stories. I recognise the diverse circumstances in which they operate and, as a result, develop tailored coaching interventions for each client, avoiding a cookie-cutter coaching approach.

- Enhancement, not Fixing: I'm likewise dedicated to enhancing my clients' development, however, with the understanding that self-development is an ongoing process. I acknowledge that my clients are not defective, down-and-out, broken, or faulty, and they are seeking coaching because they find themselves at the crossroads of self-actualisation and in a state of inertia.

- Facilitating Self-exploration: Coaching is a voyage of self-exploration of ideas, where the process is client-driven. Coaches don't instruct, lecture, teach, counsel, advise, or judge; instead, we facilitate our clients' journeys of self-exploration.

- Awakening Brilliance: Coaching, in my view, is the catalyst for reawakening and sharpening insights about the self, enabling individuals to exhibit their full brilliance in their personal and professional lives, in their relationships, and in the systems they navigate.

- Integral System Thinking: I strive to broaden my clients' understanding of phenomena by enhancing their ability to observe them from different perspectives and viewpoints.

- Best Possible Coaching Experience: In my pursuit to ensure my clients receive the best coaching experience, my coaching interventions must be founded on a robust theoretical coaching framework, sound coaching models, and empiric coaching tools while simultaneously upholding the principle of "no harm."

These are my coaching values. What are your coaching values for working with wonderful, complex human beings?

After establishing and aligning my coaching values, I embarked on an intellectual journey to develop a coaching approach—also known as a coaching practice—that considers the personal and professional challenges women face in various settings. However, *'What Women Want Coaches to Know: A Gender-Intelligent Coaching Approach'*, focuses explicitly on the experiences of women working in various sectors.

But before I share my journey to defining my coaching approach, I must admit, like many coaches, I initially used the terms coaching framework, coaching model, and coaching tools interchangeably[72].

# Coaching Lingo

Fortunately, through my coach training, I learnt that while these terms or concepts are interrelated, they represent distinct elements within the coaching approach. Moreover, I also learnt that understanding the coaching lingo is not a trivial or fancy-pansy activity but rather a vital part of establishing your distinctive coaching identity and brand, as well as a prerequisite for providing your coaching clients with the best coaching experience.

Armed with this understanding of the distinctions between coaching terms, I set out to develop the gender-intelligent coaching approach by following three key phases.

First, I developed the coaching framework, which encapsulates my values and principles, as well as selected paradigms, philosophy, and foundational theories that underpin my coaching approach[73]. The coaching framework addresses the question: What solid principles, paradigms, and theories influence my coaching intervention, and what do these principles, paradigms, and theories contribute to achieving the overarching objectives of my coaching approach?

Second, I constructed a coaching model, which represents the "how" in the coaching intervention. The coaching model's function is to structure the unfolding coaching process and direct the dialogue within the coaching sessions and the entire coaching journey[74]. Coaching models frequently include an acronym or moniker to define the key steps or stages of the coaching cycle. The coaching model answers this question: How will the coaching sessions be methodically organised and conducted, and how will the coach's inquiry guide the coaching client toward achieving their goals?

In the final phase, I curated a diverse collection of coaching tools, finding myself with an abundance of excellent options to choose from. If the coaching framework is the 'what' and the coaching model is the 'how', then the coaching tools can be understood as the 'with what.' Coaching tools are various aids and resources utilised within the coaching framework and model to support our clients in bridging the gap between their current-selves and future-selves, ultimately assisting them in achieving their desired outcomes[75]. These tools help coaches track progress, identify clients' patterns, and tailor interventions to address clients' specific coaching issues best. The coaching tools answer this question: "What aids and resources will I use to assist my clients in achieving their goals effectively?"

# NAVIGATING THE COACHING TERRAIN: APPLYING COACHING CONCEPTS IN PRACTICE

I will now illustrate these coaching terms by presenting my client, Zoë. After Zoë explored human development modalities such as therapy, counselling, and mentoring, she settled on coaching as her preferred choice. Zoë's coaching requirement was as follows: she needed to cross a turbulent river but was unsure how to accomplish it. Let's call the river "The River of Life."

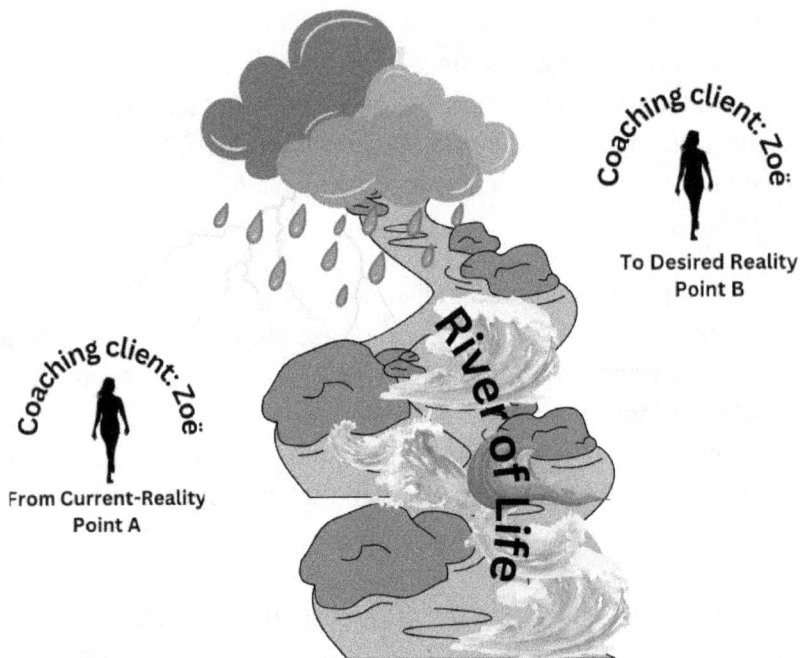

*Figure 3: Crossing the River of Life*

Zoë envisions crossing the challenging River of Life, with its turbulent waters and strong rapids. Aligned with my coaching philosophy, my utmost priority is to ensure Zoë achieves her goal of reaching the other side of the river efficiently, safely, and without harm. Conventional methods of crossing the river, like swimming or using a boat or helicopter, would prove too hazardous due to the tumultuous, crocodile-infested waters and strong winds. Therefore, we seek sustainable solutions to transport Zoë safely and efficiently across the river. What sustainable solution will we propose? We will build a bridge—our coaching approach—that will transport Zoë from the riverbank of Current-Reality to the other side, the riverbank of Desired-Reality.

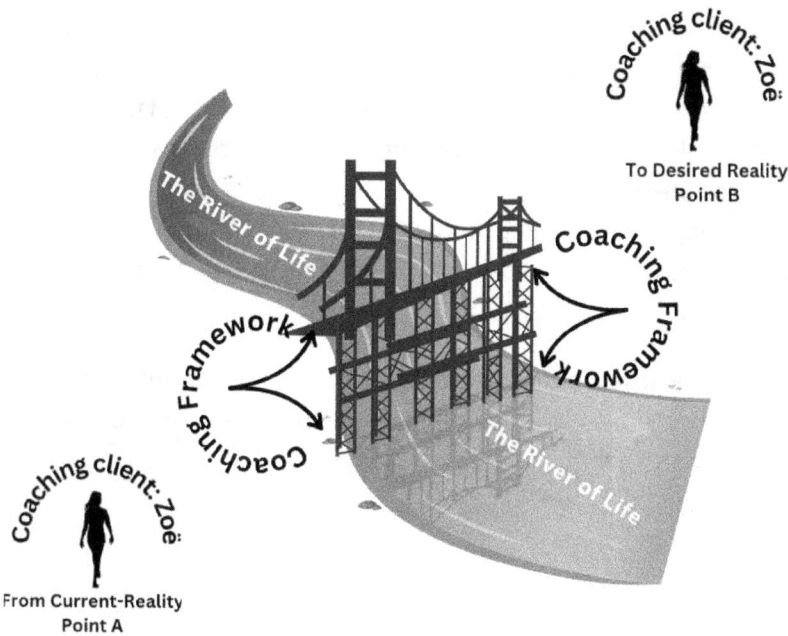

*Figure 4: Constructing a Coaching Framework*

## Coaching framework: Deck and pylons

However, before coaching Zoë to cross the bridge, the coach must construct a sturdy bridge with a stable deck and pylons. However, we know not everyone can build a bridge since it requires expertise. The viability of the bridge depends on securing it on strong foundations that meet the criteria of safety, durability, and sustainability. Therefore, the challenge we face as coaches is guaranteeing our coaching bridge is safe, durable, and sustainable.

Just as the deck and pylons provide stability and safety for a bridge, the coaching framework provides a solid theoretical foundation for the coaching approach. The efficacy of the coaching intervention derives strength from the theoretical underpinnings of the coaching framework, much as a bridge relies on sturdy pylons to withstand external pressures such as the wind or the weight of the traffic. Essentially, the coaching framework ensures that every coaching decision or coaching move the coach pursues is grounded in solid theoretical knowledge.

Adherence to a coaching framework ensures the integrity of the coaching process and illuminates the pathway toward coaching interventions that facilitate meaningful and transformative experiences for our clients.

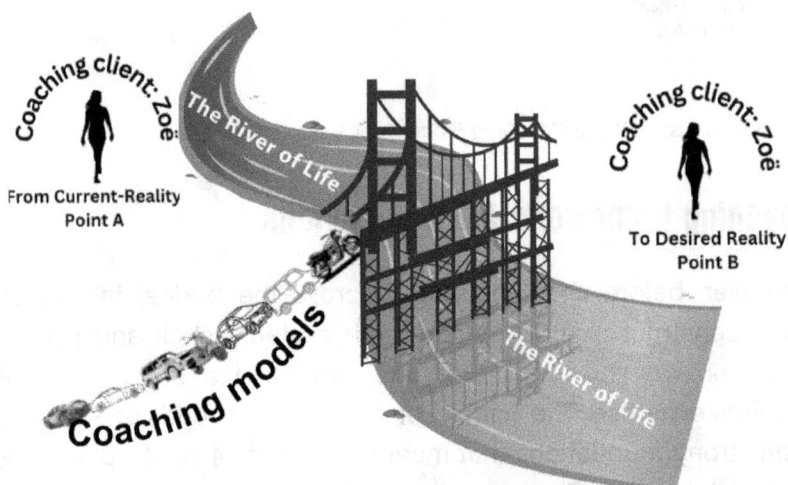

*Figure 5: The Coaching Models*

## Coaching models: Modes of transport

The modes of transport, namely the various vehicles, provide the options for the variety of coaching models that can be selected to ensure Zoë gets across the bridge efficiently and safely. In other words, how will the coaching sessions be methodically organised and conducted to ensure that the coaching intervention guides the coaching client toward achieving their goals?

## Coaching tools: Gadgets

In coaching terminology, gadgets represent the coaching tools. For instance, items like a map, GPS, music, snacks for the road trip, a chart for rest stops, a puncture kit and so forth, are tools used to assist Zoë in making her journey more efficient and tracking her progress to her destination. Similarly, in coaching, various coaching tools each serve a specific purpose in facilitating progress. I could write a book about the myriad coaching tools available, as each helps in different ways. In the coaching journey, these tools are aids and resources that coaches use to help their clients gain new perspectives and achieve their desired outcomes.

Coaching tools will be covered in chapter six, where I will share some of the tools the gender-intelligent coaching approach has lined up in its coaching toolbox.

Now that we are on the same page about the key coaching terminology, let me share how I constructed the unique gender-intelligent coaching approach.

# BAKING THE GENDER-INTELLIGENT COACHING APPROACH

Although I am about to use the comparison of baking a cake in how I went about to develop the gender-intelligent coaching approach, I must admit I cannot bake a cake to save my life! Despite reading the recipes and following the steps, or so I think, my cakes usually come out as flat as a pancake. Perhaps I needed to be more careful in how I sifted the flour or how long I mixed the ingredients, or my oven's temperature gauge may just be faulty, but most of all, I might lack creative flow in the baking department. On the other hand, my son, Sanjay, bakes flop-proof, delicious cakes. He knows the finer details of what moves he must pull to get the perfect cake. It is not just the eggs, the flour, or the butter. He hints that besides the ingredients and baking techniques, the magic lies in a hefty dose of flair and creativity, which play a vital role in making his cakes melt-in-your-mouth good.

In theory, I understand his baking process as it closely mirrors what coaches pursue in perfecting their unique coaching approach. Developing one's coaching approach requires a deep dive into the finer moves – that is, understanding the distinct coaching terms, theories, models, and tools, coupled with a big dose of learning, curiosity and flair. Moreover, it's about knowing the order of how these coaching components blend and connect in a way that facilitates a coaching intervention that is not just yummy—sorry, I am still in a baking mood—but also most beneficial for coaching clients.

Therefore, when I set out to "bake" my coaching approach explicitly suited for women, I, too, blended an eclectic mix of disciplines, of course, each rooted in sound empirical evidence. I also learned the finer details of crafting a coaching approach, ensuring my coaching intervention delivers the results women want and require. Above all, it's not just about the mixing of coaching ingredients; it's about the alchemy that happens when you combine them in just the correct order in the coaching lab!

## A Gender-Intelligent Coaching Framework That Supports Women

As noted earlier in this chapter, the coaching framework serves as the foundation of the coaching practice, akin to the structural

54

support of a bridge. It also encapsulates the coach's identity, stance, moves, and brand. Furthermore, the coaching framework embodies research and empirical findings related to the coaching focus area or what the coaching aims to resolve.

This is the exciting part of coaching; we can adopt someone else's existing coaching framework or develop our own, as I did.

Now, developing a coaching framework might sound simple, but it is an intensive process. You start the journey by scouring all theories that have found traction in the world of coaching or even go beyond the world of coaching and shine a bright light on rich resources in disciplines like neuroscience, psychology, systems thinking, future studies, etc. You examine these with one question in mind: can they contribute to the solutions my specific coaching clients are seeking? In my case, I aimed to develop a theoretical coaching framework that would provide a coaching intervention ensuring my women coaching clients are guided effectively and efficiently to achieve their desired outcomes.

I baptised my framework, the "gender-intelligent coaching framework," since the aim was to address the gender-specific challenges women encounter in various social and work contexts. I opted for this name over calling it a "women-specific coaching framework" because, although the coaching is aimed at women, the identifying coaching focus or coaching domain is on the gendered environment in which women operate.

As per the bridge analogy, where the coaching framework consists of the pillars and deck, the gender-intelligent coaching framework is built on six critical vertical pillars, each selected for its potential impact on my coaching clients. These pillars include James Flaherty's integral coaching approach, Alan Seiler's ontological coaching approach, Ken Wilber's integral theory, as well as motivational and goal performance theory, social psychology, and neuroscience theory. However, these pillars do not work in isolation; they require a unifying force. This is where gender theory steps in.

Gender theory serves as the number one pillar and acts as the unifying force by serving as the horizontal deck that holds all six selected theories in place. Specifically, gender theory addresses the gender nuances and gender dynamics our clients encounter, ensuring that the coaching approach is holistic and inclusive.

By combining these diverse theories, the gender-intelligent coaching framework coaches women clients to navigate their unique challenges and achieve their goals more effectively.

In the first iteration of this chapter, I was going to whack you over the head with my brilliance—LOL! I aimed to impress you with extensive details, ad nauseum, on each theory, spanning around sixty pages of what I thought was mind-blowing content. However, my editor wisely advised me to "kill my darlings" if I hoped to maintain your engagement. It stung a bit, but I agreed—I definitely didn't want to risk boring you to death!

I settled for the logical alternative, a comprehensive reading list. This list only requires you to flip to the reference section and read chapter five. There, I wielded a broad brushstroke to summarise the theoretical underpinning of the coaching framework. In any case, the respective theorists do a much better job of capturing the intricacies of their theories and I advise you to go directly to the source.

When crafting the gender-intelligent coaching framework, I embraced a pragmatic approach. This approach resonates with my spirit since I lean towards being a practitioner over a theoretician. A pragmatist's mode is a learning approach that hums along to the tune of pursuing action, analysing the outcomes of those actions, and if affirmative, continuing with those actions. If not, it must be recalculated, and a new course of action or actions must be pursued. However, my pragmatic mindset also favours the relationship between theory-to-practice and practice-to-theory. While a pragmatist, the spinning and spouting of theory also fascinate me.

I want to say I tapped a wand, and the gender-intelligent coaching framework whisked itself into my senses. But the truth is, it's been quite a journey, and I suspect that even after I publish this book, the journey will reveal other milestones.

The initial step is to develop the gender-intelligence coaching approach by infusing my women's development experience with various other paradigms, theories, and methods. I've said this earlier—before we can even think of coaching someone, we need to intimately know what supports our coaching intervention. When we understand why we say what we say in the coaching conversation, and why we do what we do in the coaching process, we are ready to have powerful coaching interventions.

### The Coaching Model Serves to Transport Our Coaching Clients to Their Desired Destination

As we engage in the coaching intervention, we must decide on the most efficient mode of transport to help Zoë traverse the bridge from point A, her current-self, to Point B, her desired-self.

The questions we ask are: What mode of transport is appropriate or suitable for either the conditions Zoë encounters, her way of showing up in the world and her personality? Are we using only one mode or one of many modes of transport?

In coaching, choosing coaching models is like selecting modes of transport. Deciding between using multiple models or sticking to one is crucial. The goal is to find the best methods to guide women effectively from one point to another. Mastery of different coaching models is essential for success.

Only after sorting out our coaching model can we confidently tell our clients, "Let's conquer those goals and embark on this transformative journey!"

In conclusion of this chapter, I think the best description of a professional coach is that they have a coaching strategy consisting of a coaching model underpinned by the consolidation of their experiences, possess a solid theoretical, evidence-based coaching framework, and are equipped with coaching models and tools that guide their coaching intervention. Having all these coaching components in place ensures women will not have a fly-by-the-seat-of-your-pants coaching experience. In chapter five, I discuss the theoretical underpinnings of the gender-intelligent coaching framework, but for now, let's focus on how to transport Zoë over the stable bridge by going deeper into the coaching model I have developed to serve as my transport for my women coaching clients.

## CHAPTER 4

# THE LANGUAGE OF THE W-O-M-A-N COACHING MODEL

*Women need to shift from thinking, "I'm not ready to do that," to thinking, "I want to do that, and I'll learn by doing it."*

Cheryl Sandberg
(Business Executive, Author, Founder of LeanIn.Org)

Let's get a little personal, shall we? As professional and hardworking as I am, I, too, have my share of misconceptions or presuppositions from time to time. For example, while pursuing my master's degree in coaching, my head was buzzing with a glut of information, an oversupply of reverence toward the suppliers thereof, and a diminished estimation of my potential contribution to the body of knowledge. The most challenging part was these were all organised with the clarity of a maze.

The master's course challenged this eager beaver master's student, and as with any demanding pursuit, I had moments in which I wondered, "What was I thinking?" Truth be told, there came a point when I felt so overwhelmed I tossed all my coaching toys out of the cot. This happened when the university course facilitator unequivocally stated that developing our own coaching model was an essential course prerequisite. The maze became a trap.

## The Journey to Developing a Fit-For-Women Coaching Model

I freaked! Until then, I had naively believed that coaching models were created in "theory heaven" and sent down through miraculous intervention (great scholarly books) and revealed to mortals by the anointed icons of the coaching fraternity. My only role, I thought, was to lap them up, enthusiastically infuse them into my coaching practice, and launch them into the domain of practice so that women would have amazing breakthroughs.

Jokes aside, when I realised that developing a coaching model was an essential component of the master's degree, I argued surely only coaching gurus could accomplish this since they were the ones who had it all figured out.

It was a daunting endeavour, and I would have preferred if a "guru-coach" had shown up at my doorstep to hand me his (sic) ingenious model. It is worth noting how I use the male pronoun since, at that juncture of my coaching journey, I had only been using coaching models developed by male coaches. Cringe!

With all my coaching model fretting, my imposter syndrome manifested in those precise moments. Hence, I danced again with Ms. Imposter Syndrome to the old familiar tune of "downplay your abilities." She serenaded me with her familiar questions, "Who do you think you are to build a coaching model? Do you believe you could compete with popular coaching models such as GROW, STEPPA, OSCAR, CLEAR and so on…?[76]" Previously, I would let these doubts stop me in my tracks, but now fuelled by a combination of aspiration, inspiration, and determination to earn my Master's in Coaching, I pushed back.

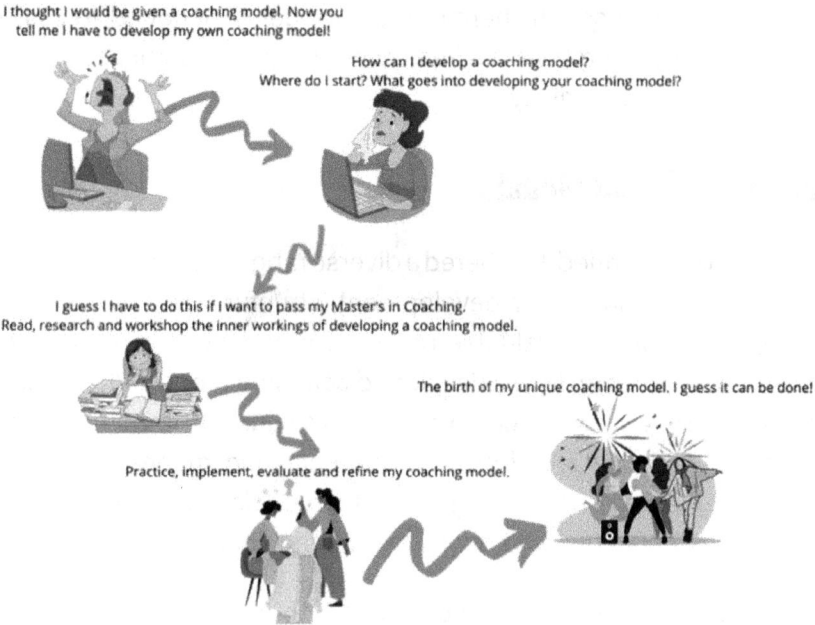

*Figure 6: What?! Must I create a coaching model?*

Now, let's move on to the process I undertook to develop my unique coaching model. Buckle up because I'm about to take you on the same bumpy ride I went through while developing my coaching model. While I wish I could claim I had one "bingo!" moment in which my coaching model was instantly born, it took me several months to construct one. As the famous Chinese philosopher Lao Tzu remarked, "The journey of a thousand miles begins with a single step."

## Defining the Purpose

The first step in developing my fit-for-women coaching model was to define its purpose. The goal was to create a coaching model explicitly designed to support women who are impacted by patriarchy, systemic racism, and sexism. The model aims to offer insights and guidance that consider the unique experiences and challenges women face, thus providing a gender-sensitive approach with the ultimate aim of enabling women's self-actualisation and self-transcendence. Furthermore, the model is designed to assist women in reaching their desired outcomes in a structured manner efficiently and effectively.

## Review Existing Models

With my goal clarified, I gathered a diverse range of coaching models to gain insight into their development, structure, and function. In doing so, I gained a valuable realisation: many coaching models are iterations of previously developed coaching models that inspire the creation of new coaching models. This insight freed me up to accept that while creating a unique coaching model, I had the liberty to lean on pre-existing coaching models and adapt them to reach my goal of building my fit-for-women coaching model.

Building my coaching model proved to be both simple and complex. On the one hand, the mechanics of creating a coaching model were easy since I was fortunate enough to know how to construct one. On the other hand, deep thinking underpinned the models I reviewed, some of which were very popular, and I have even utilised them in my coaching practice. However, my task was to determine which of these models, or parts of them, were suitable for coaching women. I concluded that while the coaching models I reviewed worked, they lacked a gendered perspective.

## Integrating the theoretical underpinnings of the Gender-Intelligent Coaching Framework

The next step was to gather the wide range of theories I previously adopted to inform my coaching approach but adapted to drive the gender-intelligent coaching approach. These theories included:

Gender Theory[77]; Flaherty's integral coaching approach[78]; Seiler's ontological coaching approach[79]; Wilber's integral theory[80], social psychology[81], motivational and goal theory[82]; and neuroscience[83].

Broadly speaking, these theories offer the perspective that we humans are the product of a complex interplay of personal, behavioural, environmental, and social influences. Any person who shows up in the world carries all these influences within them. Therefore, in the main, I am reiterating that since our world, societies, and selves are inherently gendered, coaches need to incorporate the gendered perspective into their coaching approach. I refer to this as being "gender woke" as opposed to being "gender blind".

Gender-blind or gender-neutral coaching practices are akin to doctors prescribing antibiotics without addressing the individual's specific infection and its causes. We know antibiotics are potent in fighting infections; however, using the wrong type of antibiotic can harm a patient or may fail to target specific conditions. Moreover, without identifying the antecedents that caused the infections, patients can be at risk of reinfection or never fully recovering.

Likewise, research indicates that coaching is effective. However, rather than implementing broad-spectrum coaching, we use tailor-made coaching approaches to respond to factors we know may affect women specifically at any given time.

## Adapt and Innovate

Shirley Anita Chisholm, the first African American congresswoman in the United States, said, "You don't make progress by standing on the sidelines, whimpering and complaining. You make progress by implementing ideas." This inspired me to throw my hat into the proverbial coaching ring and create a coaching model that would endeavour to take women on a journey that will allow them to reach their desired goals.

Intuitively, I knew I needed to interweave all I had learned about coaching, women's empowerment, women's development, and gender mainstreaming. Importantly, it must also be guided by my valuable years of valuable experience coaching women and understanding what worked and what did not. By marrying the most enduring theories of coaching with my rootedness in the challenges women face in a patriarchal system, I avoided simple eclecticism—a mix-and-match exercise—but sought to create a model that was integrated, had internal coherence, and was a powerful model for coaching women.

By sharing this coaching model, I aim to initiate dialogue and anticipate that the coaching tribes will contribute to refining it, ensuring it genuinely empowers women for personal and professional growth. Fortunately, and rightfully, the sequence of the steps in the model forms the mnemonic...drumroll, please... **W-O-M-A-N!**

## The W-O-M-A-N Coaching Model

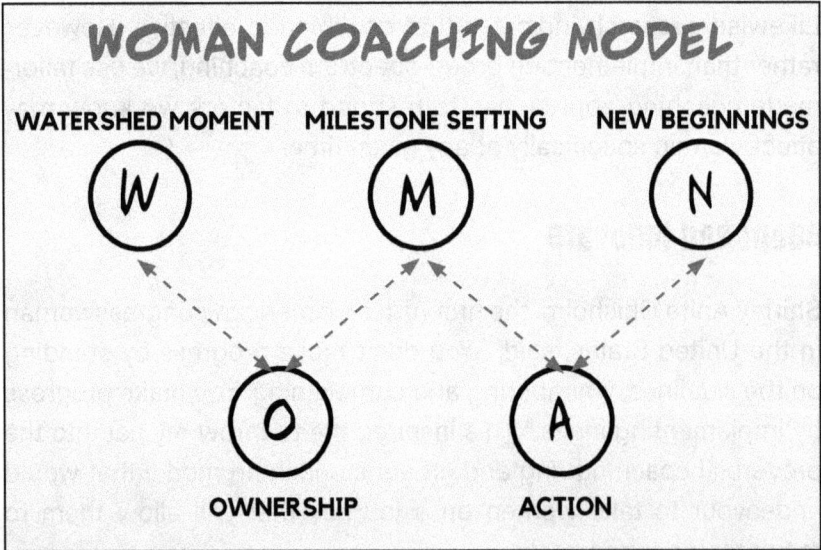

*Figure 7: W-O-M-A-N Coaching Model*

The W-O-M-A-N coaching model has five distinct phases; however, they do not necessarily need to be followed sequentially. The premise is that each phase should be explored in-depth, employing coaching tools such as deep listening, gender analysis, assessments, generative and incisive coaching questions, and a whole host of other coaching tools that could guide women in gaining insight into themselves, taking ownership of their life journey, setting milestones, taking action, and ultimately achieving their desired results.

As mentioned in chapter 3, the primary goal of any coaching model is to provide coherence in the coaching conversations and the whole coaching process. In the coaching conversations, our clients often share diverse stories, sometimes disjointed narratives, scattered thoughts, interpretations, and assumptions. The coach's role in the coaching relationship is to listen with the intent to organise and synthesise the client's narratives and facilitate clarity and structure to her thoughts and goals. The coaching model facilitates this listening process; it allows the coach to be fully present, as the steps in the coaching model guide the conversations effectively by ensuring progress towards the client's desired outcomes.

## Piloting the W-O-M-A-N Coaching Model

I piloted the W-O-M-A-N coaching model over a two year period, which has proven successful in empowering women to engage with issues in both their personal and professional lives.

Furthermore, my experiences in coaching women have shown that the line between personal and professional challenges frequently blurs. For example, a leading organisation addressing gender-based violence engaged me to coach Linda, a project leader renowned for her research talents. However, she battled considerably with public speaking and often performed poorly in presenting her research findings at public events. This had a negative impact on the organisation and, of course, caused considerable angst in

Linda's life. Linda's initial presenting coaching issue was her fear of public speaking. However, during our coaching sessions, it became clear Linda's fear of public speaking was rooted in her self-doubt about her expertise and leadership capacity. Research on self-attribution indicates that women often find it challenging to own and present their expertise because they tend to have low self-attribution. Consequently, the coaching focused on overcoming low self-attribution, building her self-confidence, developing her leadership voice, and enhancing her leadership presence. Linda received coaching not only to overcome her fear of public speaking but also to address the root causes of this fear. After eight coaching sessions, she not only conquered her fear of public speaking but also gained confidence in asserting her expertise in both her professional and personal life. She now presents herself as an effective leader, a research expert on gender-based violence, and has taken agency in all areas of her life.

As evidenced by Linda's journey, the effectiveness of the W-O-M-A-N coaching model extends beyond addressing surface-level challenges; it is all about going beyond the surface issue and getting to know what lies beneath.

## The Phases of the W-O-M-A-N Coaching Model

To provide a comprehensive understanding of the W-O-M-A-N coaching model, I will outline each phase and then delve into detailed explanations of its elements. By doing so, I aim to ensure a thorough understanding of their importance and how they contribute to the coaching journey.

## Dear Coach Letters

Additionally, I believe it is important to incorporate and amplify the voices of the women we coach. Through the "Dear Coach" letters, these women's voices will validate their experiences, insights, needs, and priorities. These letters are based on feedback

I received from my coaching clients, as well as research on the impact of coaching on women. They also include findings on how gender bias and stereotypes affect women and how coaches can use these insights to tailor their approach. These letters will offer valuable guidance to coaches who coach women, enriching the authenticity of the coaching process. Hence the book's title, "What Women Want Coaches to Know".

## Guidepost for Coaches

Finally, I will provide guideposts to assist coaches in navigating each phase effectively. These guideposts will offer practical advice on utilising tools and principles to support the women client's coaching journey.

## Phase one: The WATERSHED Moment

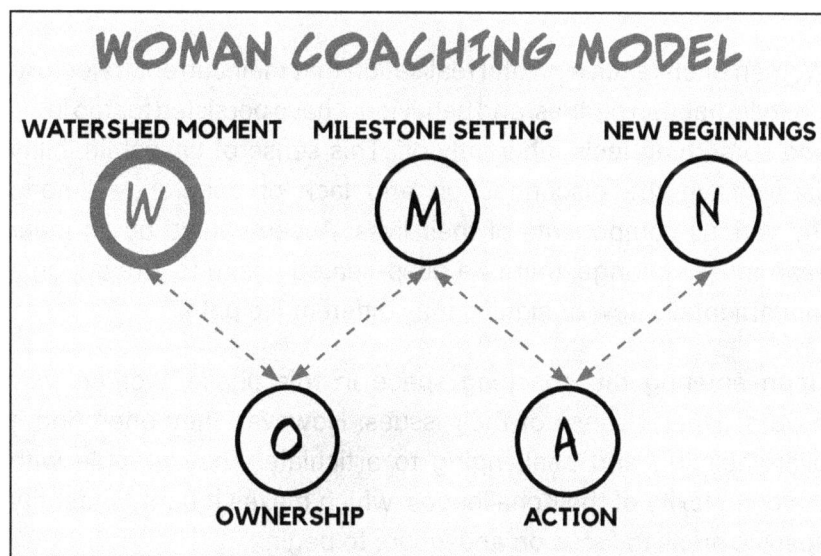

WOMAN COACHING MODEL

WATERSHED MOMENT     MILESTONE SETTING     NEW BEGINNINGS

W     M     N

O     A

OWNERSHIP     ACTION

The watershed moment is that insightful realisation—an "aha moment," if you will—when an individual, having exhausted her inner resources, recognises the need to seek the guidance of a professional. In this scenario, they have reached out to a coach—you—to assist them in making sense of this moment in their lives.

This pivotal moment can occur in an instant, setting the stage for women to embark on a transformative shift in their life's trajectory. People use various terms to describe this profound moment, such as serendipity, fate, karma, destiny, providence, awakening, and an unexpected turn of events. However, "watershed" best encapsulates the idea that there was a journey, uninterrupted and unfiltered, then interrupted or constrained, leading to newfound clarity.

I refer to it as the watershed moment, which essentially signifies the point at which a specific life issue moves from the unconscious to the conscious, from the possibly unknown to the known, from the unspoken to the stated, from the opaque to the transparent, and from the generally accepted as normality to the perplexingly abnormal.

Women often reach a pivotal realisation that their current trajectory, lifestyle, habits, routines, and behaviours have persisted for too long, and something feels inherently off. This sense of unsustainability stems from the disconnection and lack of coherence among the various components of their lives. Accompanied by an inner yearning for change, there's a deep-seated desire to embark on a fundamentally new or significantly different life path.

Upon entering the coaching space in this phase, women may have a general sense of their issues. However, they often find it overwhelming and challenging to articulate. They grapple with the complexity of their challenges, which makes it hard to identify specific areas to focus on and where to begin.

Moreover, they may need clarification about whether coaching is the appropriate solution. This is where coaches play a crucial role. By offering a reflective space, coaches support women navigating through their uncertainties and gaining clarity. It's essential to reassure them that coaching provides a safe environment for them to take ownership of their lives.

As coaches, it's our duty to grasp the importance of these watershed moments. By exploring their life stories and the reasons behind seeking coaching, we help women realise the weight of this defining moment and clarify their goals. Armed with this insight, coached women can start their journey with clear direction and determination.

All I say to my women clients is, "Welcome to a renewed lease on life!" Let me illustrate this with the example of a  woman leader I coached. For years, she found herself repeatedly admitted to a mental rehab facility because of burnout and breakdowns caused by unsustainable work practices. This pattern persisted for years until one morning, following yet another admission, she realised she could no longer continue down this life path. Not only was it detrimental to her well-being, personal life, and work life, but it also set a bad example for her colleagues and two daughters. Following her release from the facility, she contracted me to coach her. One of our coaching goals was to empower her to be assertive, to say "no" without feeling guilty, and to reclaim her boundaries in order to foster sustainable work practices, outsource some of her tasks, and join a supportive network of other women leaders who could provide her with a space for reflection, share the challenges she is facing, and celebrate and share her successes.

This example showcases the transformative power of the watershed moment and the subsequent journey. By recognising the need for change and seeking support, individuals can break free from negative patterns and habits and make positive strides towards personal and professional growth.

Aside from this example, would you consider this a life coaching or a business-executive coaching issue? The gender-intelligent coaching approach finds the divide between life and business coaching problematic. The gender-intelligent coaching approach postulates that we cannot have a strict, impenetrable wall between life coaching and business coaching issues. This perspective needs to be updated, as it is nearly impossible to separate and compartmentalise one's personal and professional lives effectively despite our best efforts. This is especially true for women, who primarily handle the three C's—caregiving, cleaning, and cooking—and frequently balance their personal and professional obligations without having the option to prioritise one over the other. Therefore, to maximise the potential to address both personal and professional goals, we need a more holistic coaching approach.

## *What Women Want Coaches to Know*

Dear Coach,

Thank you for coaching me through my watershed moment. I sensed a shared understanding in our initial coaching sessions, perhaps drawn from your personal watershed moments. Throughout our coaching journey, several aspects of your approach have deeply resonated with me.

I had a pivotal realisation: I almost overlooked my watershed moment. It wasn't until I sought coaching that I recognised how close I came to disregarding it and moving on. Had I not paid attention, I would have eventually looked back and regretted not recognising its significance. How many women navigate the world with regret for not acknowledging their own watershed moments?

Your emphasis on growth rather than dwelling on perceived failures or setbacks has been incredibly empowering. You've consistently acknowledged my accomplishments and competence, instilling a renewed sense of self-worth.

I've appreciated your encouragement to trust my intuition and embrace this watershed moment as the beginning of a new chapter.

I have recognised that the prevailing traditional fairy tales often portray damsels in distress, relying on external rescuers, usually a prince, to rescue them from every predicament, whether it's awakening them with a kiss, finding their missing shoe, rescuing them on a white horse, and so forth. These tales rarely depict princesses who save themselves; moreover, our society seldom tells alternative fairy tales of women warriors who save themselves and others. In our coaching journey, we're challenging this narrative and realising the importance of self-reliance. I must reclaim myself as my own warrior because I thrive when I advocate for myself. Your support in articulating the need for strategies to resist stereotypes and discrimination has been enlightening and empowering. You've provided a safe and supportive space for me to explore innovative solutions and navigate obstacles on my journey as my accountability partner.

Your commitment to celebrating my uniqueness, successes, and transformation without judgment has inspired me. Through coaching, I've realised I can safely entrust my vision to myself.

With heartfelt gratitude,

Wise Woman

## A Guidepost to Coaches

Coaches who find themselves in this phase of coaching should note the following:

- Transition from Uncertainty to Clarity: In this phase, the coach seeks to empower women to first determine if coaching is the appropriate modality for them. This may include encouraging women to assess whether coaching aligns with their needs and if there is a connection between themselves and the coach. However, it is crucial to recognise coaching is not always the sole or primary solution for every individual's needs. If you seldom refer clients to other human care modalities, it is time to build your network of trusted professionals, including therapists, medical practitioners, and other specialists. This network ensures that you can provide clients with reliable referrals tailored to their specific needs. From my coaching experience, women often neglect self-care, and particularly their health needs. Part of the coaching process is ensuring the whole person is being addressed.

- Utilising the Skills of "Bracketing": Coaches possess a remarkable talent known as "bracketing." So, please switch it on! This superpower skill involves setting aside preconceived notions and biases, quieting our inner chatter, and engaging in deep listening. By bracketing ourselves, we step into the client's shoes—whether they're navigating life in killer high heels, brand new boots, well-worn running shoes, sturdy pumps, or even comfy Crocs (no judgment here!). By practising bracketing, coaches can create a non-judgmental space for clients. This deep listening guides coaches to be fully present and empathetic, making the client feel heard and understood and, ultimately, fostering a more meaningful and transformative coaching experience.

- Asking Generative and Incisive Questions: The power of coaching lies in asking generative and incisive questions that open up meaningful and insightful conversations. These questions encourage clients to deeply explore their thoughts, feelings, and motivations, facilitating self-awareness and personal growth. Generative questions are open-ended and exploratory, allowing clients to consider new perspectives and possibilities. For example, "What would your ideal life look like if you could remove all obstacles?" This type of question encourages clients to dream and envision broader possibilities without immediate constraints. Generative questions inspire innovation and forward-thinking by fostering an environment of curiosity and open-mindedness. Incisive questions, on the other hand, are sharp and focused, cutting through superficial responses to reach the core of the client's concerns. For instance, "What is the one fear stopping you from pursuing your goal?" Incisive questions often lead to breakthroughs by challenging limiting beliefs or assumptions. Effective coaching requires balancing these questioning techniques to create a supportive and challenging environment. Ultimately, asking the right questions can lead to transformative insights.

- Use Assessment Tools: Assessment tools are a vital part of the coaching toolbox. Therefore, using assessment forms in the watershed phase provides both the coach and women coaching clients with deeper insights into their lives and offers objective measures to evaluate progress. Examples of assessments worth exploring include the Satisfaction with Life Scale, the Wheel of Life Scale, the Enneagram, the VIA Inventory of Strengths, or any other tools deemed appropriate.

- Gender-Intelligent Coaching: Women do not exist in isolation, and therefore, it is essential for coaching to recognise the socio-political and gendered landscape that influences women's lives. Understand their relationships, environments with people and systems are often laden with complexities and challenges unique to their gender. Be aware that many women find themselves in environments exposing them to discourses, ideologies, and situations that are disadvantageous, subjecting them to biases and discrimination and thus hindering them from reaching their full potential.

- Metaphors and Analogies: Pay close attention to the metaphors and analogies the client uses to describe their situations. These provide invaluable insight into how women perceive, feel, and experience their situations. For example, they might describe themselves as being in "stormy waters", "stuck on a treadmill that does not have an off switch," "drowning in work", or "lost in a forest without an exit plan." These metaphors offer valuable insights, vividly illustrating their struggles and guiding your approach.

- Body Language, Words and Emotions: Gender-intelligent coaching involves attentive observation of women's body language by paying close attention to their posture, gestures, and facial expressions. Body language can reveal unspoken feelings and attitudes, providing insights into a client's comfort level, confidence, and openness to change. The words women choose to describe their experiences, challenges, and aspirations are crucial indicators of their internal states. Gender-intelligent coaches listen for patterns in language that may reflect societal conditioning or internalised gender norms. For example, women might downplay their achievements or use qualifiers that undermine their confidence ("I think I can" instead of "I can"). Emotions play a pivotal role in the coaching process, particularly for women who may experience a range of feelings influenced by their personal and professional lives. Coaches should be adept at identifying and validating these emotions, creating a safe space for women to express themselves fully.

- Support and Accountability: Coaching aims to provide women with a positive and meaningful experience throughout their coaching journey. One element of fostering a positive and meaningful experience is serving as their trusted accountability partner and creating a safe space that supports their progress and growth.

- Handle Emotions with Care: For coaches, our clients' tears, or what I call "emotional salt water," do not signify weakness. Often, these emotional expressions indicate a determination to overcome obstacles and readiness to embark on their transformative life journey. And yes, coaches are trained to handle emotions with empathy and professionalism!

- Uphold Trust and Ensure Confidentiality: Confidentiality and trust are the cornerstones of coaching. As a coach, it is imperative to uphold these principles and never violate your clients' trust. This brings me to a critical issue—my pet peeve—coaches who break confidentiality by using their clients to advertise their coaching business. I always ask coaches, "Have you ever seen a therapist ask their clients to sing their praises or post photos of their clients publicly?" So, what's up with coaches? Breaking ethics codes and confidentiality by exposing our clients via requesting testimonials and posting photos of our clients on social media? Is this not a confidential relationship where our clients are provided with a space where they do not have to worry their business will serve as public fodder? Even if a client agrees to promote your coaching services, consider alternative methods, such as the option of anonymous testimonials. Maintaining confidentiality is paramount, and coaches should ensure their marketing practices respect the privacy and trust of their clients. Yes, I am very serious about this!

- Empower women: Our role as coaches is to coach women to recognise their worth, their right to pursue their life goals, and their right to pursue this journey with confidentiality, respect, and integrity.

## Phase two: OWNERSHIP Phase

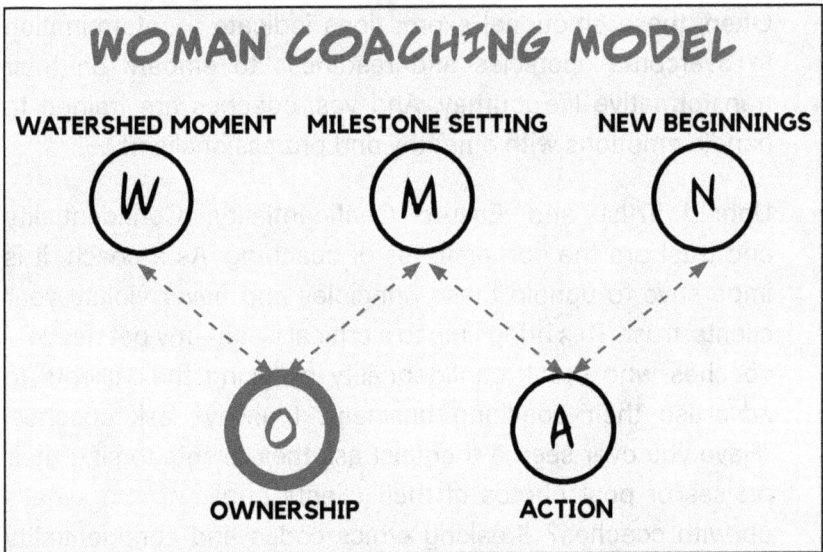

Women who experience discrimination, marginalisation, or prejudice may feel alienated from both external power sources and their own capabilities. This disconnects causes individuals to doubt their innate self-worth. This might lead to their inability to recognise and utilise their inherent potential and talents, which in turn fosters feelings of doubt and insecurity. Consequently, faced with challenges of discrimination, marginalisation, or disempowerment, some individuals may opt to relinquish control, leading them to deny their agency in the face of adversity. This can result in a cycle of self-doubt and diminished self-worth.

Effective coaching interventions must, when coupled with the watershed moment, begin to ignite the spark of inner agency. The coaching goal is to develop the woman's self-efficacy and her trust in herself to take ownership of the coaching journey since she is able to do so.

The ownership phase catalyses women to embrace their role as stewards in their own lives. Essentially, it entails a coaching relationship where women acknowledge and take charge of their potential, achievements, and outcomes. This phase ignites their intrinsic agency, a key ingredient for women to transform their lives and strive for their best selves.

While there are several distinctions between therapy, mentoring, and coaching, one crucial aspect I underscore here is the paramount importance of the coaching client taking ownership of the coaching journey. It is not simply about waiting for the coach to deliver; it is the coaching client who gains the confidence to realise they are captains of their own lives and the captain in the coaching journey. Assuming ownership of the coaching process propels women towards independently achieving their desired outcomes.

As previously stated, coaching isn't about fixing women or providing advice; coaches are not ultracrepidarians! Instead, coach and client embrace a learning mindset, cultivating a coach-client collaboration rooted in reflection, action, review, and continuous learning.

It is widely recognised that coaching's true impact is seen when our clients commit to self-propulsion and self-regulation on their journey. This level of ownership empowers women to direct their growth and development, resulting in long-term and sustainable outcomes. By embracing this mindset, women can unlock their full potential and succeed on their terms.

### *What Women Want Coaches to Know*

Dear Coach,

I wanted to share with you how transformative the ownership phase has been for me. It has been an eye-opening experience since the insights I gained have genuinely been enlightening.

Here are some insights I acquired during the ownership phase:

Oops! I get it now. No one is going to save me! Now, that was a hard one to accept, but it has meant I have now placed the locus of control within myself.

I appreciate you bringing to my attention the research findings indicating men tend to attribute their success to their innate qualities, talents, skills, and diligence while attributing their failures to external factors. In contrast, women are more likely to attribute their success to external factors such as the team, environment, or even a mentor or coach and tend to blame themselves for any failures. This pattern shows we outsource our success and internalise our failures. This insight enabled me to reframe my successes and failures.

I was laughing about your reference to the "failure altars" that we lovingly stock instead of cherishing our success. My insight now is that our "failure altars" don't define us but serve as lessons for growth. By focusing on my accomplishments and developing self-efficacy, I have grown.

The coaching focused on the importance of developing my self-confidence muscle by feeding it praise for my achievements. I walk more confidently in my leadership shoes now, and it has empowered me to take ownership of my successes and learn from my mistakes.

Developing an inventory of my achievements has renewed my sense of purpose and energy, empowering me to face challenges with renewed strength.

I will credit myself for my coaching success and trust you won't view it as arrogance!

Yeah, I know the ball is in my court now, and I am ready to play.

With gratitude,

Wise Woman

## A Guidepost to Coaches

For coaches navigating the ownership phase:

- Assess Readiness for Ownership: Begin by assessing the women's readiness to assert agency and ownership of their lives. These assessments provide invaluable coaching opportunities, enabling women to embrace ownership and responsibility for the coaching journey. It does not have to be a fancy assessment. Just ask the client, on a scale of one to five, "Who is the most important person in the coaching relationship?" Another helpful analogy to illustrate the concept of ownership is to compare it to running one's own marathon, emphasising the significance of the individual running the race by setting one's own pace and crossing the finish line independently.

- Emphasise Accountability, Not Judgment: Use appropriate occasions to emphasise your role as an accountability partner rather than a judgmental figure. While evaluating progress is important, coaching sharpens and fosters self-reflection. Take time to determine what obstacles prevent the client from adopting and pursuing new behaviours. Remember, our role is not to crack the whip but to use it as a tool to point to the possible ways that bring the client closer to her desired self.

- Clarify Your Role as a Thinking Partner: Clarify your role as a thinking partner by actively collaborating with clients to explore new ways of presenting themselves to the world. Encourage open communication and brainstorming sessions to foster creativity, innovation, and problem-solving. Foster an environment where women feel empowered to take risks and push boundaries in pursuit of their goals.

- Act as a Mirror: The coach's role is to act as a mirror, revealing concealed behaviour patterns that detract from the coaching clients' lives. Coach women to recognise and understand these patterns by enabling them to make deliberate decisions that align with their goals, values, and principles.

By embodying these principles, coaches can create a supportive and empowering environment that facilitates women's growth, self-discovery, and taking ownership of their lives.

## Phase three: <u>MI</u>LESTONES

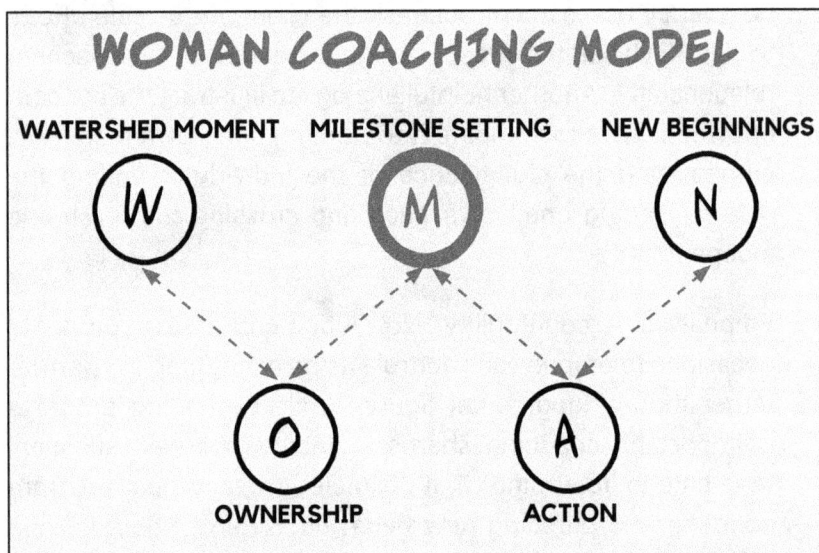

WOMAN COACHING MODEL

WATERSHED MOMENT     MILESTONE SETTING     NEW BEGINNINGS

( W )     ( M )     ( N )

( O )     ( A )

OWNERSHIP     ACTION

The natural progression from a moment of revelation (the watershed phase) to the beginnings of agency (the ownership phase) often brings forth a surge of passion and enthusiasm. While this enthusiasm is encouraging, it demands careful guidance, nurturing, pacing, and assessment. The milestone phase involves tracking progress along the path towards reaching the goal.

Furthermore, it pins down specific schedules for the completion of critical tasks, which will assist the client in assessing whether they are making progress towards the goal. Milestones help break down larger goals into smaller, more manageable steps, offering checkpoints to evaluate progress and adjust strategies as needed. Importantly, these progress markers serve to motivate clients by celebrating their accomplishments along the path to their desired goals.

Drawing on the analogy of a marathon (although I've never personally run one), I find inspiration in the dedication and resilience of marathon runners. In the coaching context, I'm equally inspired by women who, when resolving to change their lives, demonstrate commitment and grit in their pursuits. It is, therefore, crucial for the coach to understand the state of readiness and the energy levels of the coaching client and to develop milestones of measured and sequential achievements to prevent either despondency when a frenetic pace does not yield commensurate results or, worse, burnout when the energy is expended before any significant progress is made.

The milestone phase of coaching should provide five crucial insights for women, similar to the course flags and mile markers on a marathon route:

- Direction: Indicates which course they intend to take and whether they are on the right track.

- Progress: Keeps track of how far they've come and how much further they need to go.

- Pace: Indicates whether they are running too fast or too slow to achieve their goal.

- Time: Permits clients to plan according to the allotted time to accomplish their goals.

- Destination: The destination indicates when the client achieved their goal.

Milestone markers empower runners to make the necessary adjustments to finish the race successfully within the allotted time. Similarly, the milestone phase represents the markers illuminating the path women must follow to achieve their aspirations.

Goal-setting is an area where coaching truly shines—setting milestones to achieve one's goals and developing strategies to achieve them is the superpower of coaches. While motivation and goal attainment theories are beyond this book's scope, it's worth mentioning that abundant reading material is available on goal attainment.

In summary, the key fundamentals to remember in goal-setting and achievement are:

- Set timeframes.

- Track progress and adjust actions accordingly.

- Celebrate achievements.

During this phase, coaches often quote Albert Einstein, who famously said, "The definition of insanity is doing the same thing over and over again and expecting different results." This underscores the importance of ensuring our coaching clients do not fall into old habits but stick to the milestones they have set for themselves. Notably, the milestones are set according to the capacity of the coaching client and contextual factors. Flexibility in achieving goals is crucial, and course correction is the aim of coaching during the milestone phase.

## *What Women Want Coaches to Know*

Dear Coach,

We're thrilled and so ready to achieve a new way of being!

You understood my reasons for seeking coaching and validated my thoughts and feelings. The listening and thinking partnership we've created has laid a solid foundation for me to embark on our journey towards achieving our goals.

Thank you for guiding me to a point where I am ready for the journey of reflection, learning, action, adaptation, and the entire cycle of growth.

You inspired me with Pema Chodron's words, "A warrior begins to take responsibility for the direction of her life." I am determined and resolved to move forward in this phase.

You cautioned me that, although there is more clarity, the coaching space is where I can construct and reconstruct my stories, enabling me to let go of the past and chart the best path towards my desired future outcomes.

Instead of endorsing the misguided notion of "fake it until you make it," you emphasised the importance of authenticity, encouraging me to pursue my goals while being true to my genuine self rather than pretending to be someone I am not. This approach boosted my self-confidence since my achievements are built on honesty and self-awareness.

Recognising my juggling act of multiple responsibilities, you've coached me to permit myself to prioritise self-care without guilt, understanding it's a powerful way to bounce back from any setbacks.

Your goal-driven approach has sparked my eagerness to explore the science behind goal-setting.

We have worked hard to set and recognise that milestones can serve as motivators to stay on course. I love the fact that you foreground my past accomplishments when I feel under-accomplished.

Thank you for coaching women to define ourselves to ourselves and others, emphasising the power of positive internal self-talk.

Your incisive gender-dynamics questions have also allowed me to don my gender lenses to diagnose challenges I am faced with in the workplace, and I am learning to manage the symptoms of living in a gendered world.

Your straightforward yet empathetic and compassionate approach is a truly invaluable coaching skill.

Finally, thank you for not dictating what I must or should do but instead providing me with the space to set my milestones and adopt strategies to enable me to reach them. This approach may significantly increase the likelihood of achieving my goals with you acting as my accountability partner.

With appreciation,

Wiser Woman

## *A Guidepost to Coaches*

As women progress through the ownership phase, they've painted a sweeping canvas of their lives, acknowledging the importance of their watershed moments. The milestone phase is the opportune time to review this canvas, coaching them to define what they want to achieve and by when. Your role during this phase is pivotal in ensuring clients develop actionable plans that result in their desired outcomes.

- Coaching for Goal-setting: Their plans may encompass a spectrum of aspirations, from accomplishments to envisioned feelings and the motivations behind them. This is where your coaching expertise in goal-setting shines. Demonstrate mastery in crafting SMART (specific, measurable, achievable, relevant, timely) or CLEAR (collaborative, limited, emotional, appreciable, refinable) goals. Fully understand the common hurdles women face in goal achievement, backed by researched and informed discussions, and outline strategies to overcome these obstacles.

- Readiness Assessment: Utilise various techniques and tools to assess women's readiness to bridge the gap between their set goals and the path ahead. Ask probing questions to stimulate deep reflection and generate insights. For example, inquire about the rationale behind their chosen path, potential obstacles, and the emotional impact of achieving their goals.

- Accountability Partner: Be steadfast in holding women accountable to the goals they have set for themselves. Your role isn't merely to appease but to ensure tangible progress and achievement. That is what you get paid for as a coach! Thus, continuously reinforce their talents, successes, and accomplishments to bolster their confidence and motivation. Remind them they possess the skills and capabilities needed to accomplish their objectives and goals.

- Recognising Commitment: Indicators that women have embraced the goal-setting plan include shifts in body language, positive language usage, seeking clarification through additional questions, and exhibiting enthusiasm for their potential achievements

- Embracing these principles helps establish a supportive environment for women to grow, discover themselves, and take charge of their goals.

## Phase four: ACTION

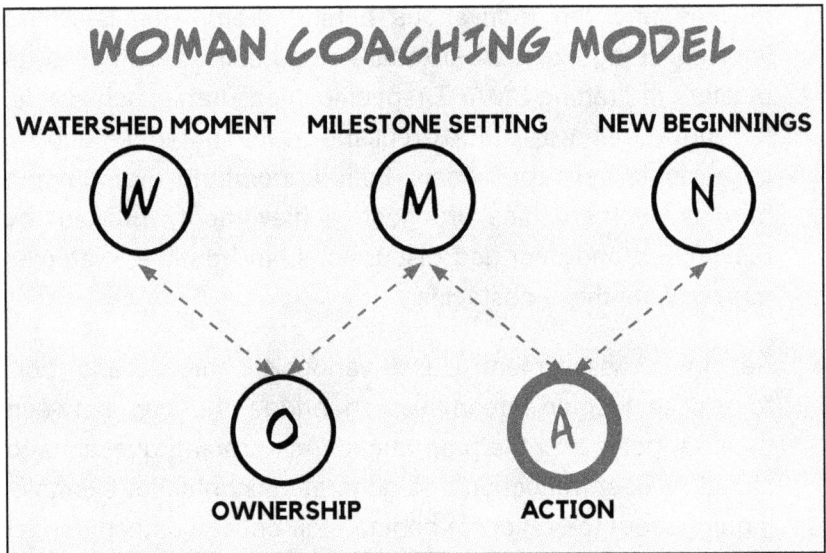

**WOMAN COACHING MODEL**

WATERSHED MOMENT  MILESTONE SETTING  NEW BEGINNINGS

W  M  N

O  A

OWNERSHIP  ACTION

Magical, and then some!

Even magical milestones, while alluring when written down, require animation—they must be brought to life with actionable steps—and action needs an action plan! The watershed phase sparked the impetus for the ownership phase, which in turn generated the milestones. However, the milestones can often serve as the cemetery of transformation – these milestones can become the place where transformation efforts can stall.

Hence, the importance of the action phase of the W-O-M-A-N coaching model. In this phase, a remarkable transformation takes place within our clients. This phase bridges the vast gap between insight and action by weaving together the threads of insight, knowledge, and action. For example, consider someone who wants to write a book. They know they need to develop a writing schedule and write consistently. Despite understanding this, there is often a gap between knowing what to do and doing it. Hands up if you can relate to this dilemma of "knowing what to do yet feeling stuck when it is time to act."

This is where coaching jumps into our golden action chariot. Thousands of books have been published on people who have great insights but fail to act on them - yes, on how to get people to act! Through coaching, we serve as action companions for women. It is not about forcing change or imposing a rigid strategy. Instead, it is a process that empowers clients to gain self-awareness and then take diligent and meaningful action. The primary objective in the action phase of coaching women is to envision and enact substantial action that propels them forward on their path to success. This is the fundamental heartbeat of being a true coach, and it requires knowledge of the scientific basis of human growth and what drives behaviour.

In the action phase, coaches must coach clients in turning resolve into tangible action. We all know too well how often clients can relinquish a cherished goal and live with regret, having abandoned it. This is why coaches need the skill to coach clients to transform resolve into practice, and clients need the doggedness to see the plan to fruition.

Gender-intelligent coaching is about building women's capacity to gain profound insights into themselves, their behaviour, and their habits. In addition, coaching involves women taking action to propel themselves forward. Action emerges when women exhibit willingness, curiosity, and positivity while embracing transformative change. However, self-efficacy, or the unshakeable confidence in one's talents, is the most important motivator for acting. It includes the knowledge that achieving success requires hard work and determination.

The coach's role is to coach for positive causal attribution and foster self-efficacy. It requires instilling the belief that they can accomplish their objectives through hard work and overcoming significant obstacles. This is the phase for active experimentation, evaluating their actions, and altering their plans if the expected results are not being met. Since real change and goal achievement are rarely easy, the coach should encourage women to practice patience, transform it into resilience, and keep track of their actions, as this may lead to unexpected moments of self-discovery.

Why, you may ask, are these self-discovery moments so important? Previously our clients used to react and try to move at breakneck speed to do it all, but now they're discovering the power of proactive action. Instead of reflexive responses, they are circumspect and respond with intention and renewed belief that what they need to achieve is within reach. This is a particularly vital skill when encountering discrimination and bias. Typically, when we are confronted with prejudice and discriminatory behaviour, we reflexively fight, flee, freeze, or faint. But now that our clients are more aware of these protective responses when faced with a similar challenging situation, they are equipped to respond differently – fearless, forthright, and with fortitude.

As they experience different results, their confidence and self-belief are enhanced. They proceed with the enthusiasm they thought they had lost. Their demeanour transforms—they walk taller, talk more confidently, and their attitudes shift positively. They hesitate less and assert more. They cut to the chase and focus on solutions rather than problems. They don the armour of confidence, shedding self-doubt.

While the action phase is impressive, it poses challenges. Lack of readiness in the woman client could hinder progress. Continued coaching is vital to build inner strength, offer support, spark inspiration, and explore new strategies to advance. Besides celebrating milestones, a practical action plan is crucial to arm women with tools to tackle potential obstacles. Anticipating and addressing these hurdles beforehand is key to prevention.

In the gender-intelligent coaching approach, in the action phase, women coaching clients are introduced to the concept of overcoming challenges through a powerful poem by Portia Nelson titled *"There's a Hole in My Sidewalk: The Romance"*[84]; a poem that deals with the power of habit and challenges.

**Chapter One**

I walk down the street.
There is a deep hole in the sidewalk.
I fall in.
I am lost... I am helpless.
It isn't my fault.
It takes forever to find a way out.

**Chapter Two**

I walk down the same street.
There is a deep hole in the sidewalk.
I pretend I don't see it.
I fall in again.
I can't believe I am in the same place.
But it isn't my fault.
It still takes a long time to get out.

**Chapter Three**

I walk down the same street.
There is a deep hole in the sidewalk.

I see it is there.
I still fall in... it's a habit.
My eyes are open.
I know where I am.
It is my fault... I get out immediately.

**Chapter Four**

I walk down the same street.
There is a deep hole in the sidewalk.
I walk around it.

**Chapter Five**

I walk down another street.

Clients can gain insight from this poem by learning the following lessons:

- *Insight 1:* The first step to overcoming challenges is awareness of their existence. Initially, the individual falls into the hole without understanding the cause.

- *Coaching Application:* Encourage clients to recognise and acknowledge their challenges or repeated patterns of behaviour. Awareness is the first step toward change.

- *Insight 2:* Responsibility for one's actions is crucial for personal growth. Initially, the individual believes the situation is not their fault, but gradually they accept responsibility.

- *Coaching Application:* Coach clients to accept accountability for their choices and actions. This shift empowers them to make proactive changes rather than feeling like victims of circumstances.

- *Insight 3:* Repeatedly encountering the same problem can lead to learning and growth. Initially, the individual continues to fall into the hole but learns to navigate it more effectively over time.

- *Coaching Application:* Help clients understand that mistakes are part of the learning process. Encourage them to reflect on their experiences and extract valuable lessons to avoid repeating the same mistakes.

- *Insight 4:* True change involves altering one's path or approach to avoid recurring problems. Eventually, the individual chooses to walk down a different street.

- *Coaching Application:* Support clients in identifying new strategies or paths to help them achieve their goals more effectively. Emphasise the importance of adaptability and the willingness to change course when necessary.

## What Women Want Coaches to Know

Dear Coach,

Phew, what a journey it's been! I'll confess, I had some preconceived notions when I first learned about coaching. I thought it might be all fluffy, upbeat pop psychology, where all I get is a pat on the back and an encouraging, "you go, girl!" and motivational fluff. But little did I know how much behavioural science and empirical evidence support how you propel me forward.

I appreciate your confidence in me, uncovering my innate talents, igniting the fire within, and propelling me toward my goals.

I'll admit I was worried about how you'd perceive me when I have set goals, but then at the follow-up session have to admit that I have not achieved the goals I had agreed to. But despite my concerns, we found positive insights even in our perceived failures. I appreciated you reminded me that if achieving the goals we set was so easy, the coaching profession would be out of business—LOL!

Of course, I wonder if you will always remain motivational, supportive, non-judgmental, and insightful throughout this coaching process. Are we still allowed to have watershed moments when things don't quite work out? Can we count on you to coach us to re-centre?

I've heard that we don't have to worry about this as you are naturally empathetic, that you understand that changing behavior is challenging, and that the world can be unkind to those who pursue a new path. We've also heard that because you know that strong women deserve to be pushed to bring out their inner strength, your magic lies in coaching women like us to achieve, just like intense pressure causes carbon to turn into diamonds.

I'm concerned that despite my newfound insights and strategies to navigate the journey, I may still stumble into potholes and struggle to find my way out. In those moments, I'll rely on you to ask those magical, incisive questions that will help me extricate myself from these potholes. Yes, I know the goal of the coaching is that I exit the process by taking action, reflecting on the action, learning from that action and taking action again on a rinse-and-repeat cycle.

Having you in my corner, acknowledging the challenges of a gendered world with its negative stereotypes, sexism, and naysayers, makes me feel more confident. Even with the occasional fears and insecurities, I trust the tools you've equipped me with to navigate "gender imbalance".

Thank you for accompanying me on this transformative journey. I eagerly anticipate your continued empowerment as I unlock my potential to create my desired life.

Warmest regards,

Much Wiser Woman

## A Guidepost to Coaches

Coaches who find themselves in the action phase of the W-O-M-A-N coaching model should:

Ensure that the women you are coaching have clarity on the goals they are working towards before launching the plan into action. Continue asking probing questions to uncover the underlying motivations and aspirations behind their goals. For instance, "What would achieving this goal mean for you?" or "Why is this goal important to you right now?"

- **Prioritise Goals:** Proceed with the most immediate need or goal. If any goals are interdependent, decide which goal should be addressed first before proceeding to the next.

- **Coaching Tools:** Utilise coaching tools that promote and track action.

- **Scenario Planning and Visualisation:** Encourage women to engage in scenario planning and visualisation by always motivating them to explore different ideas for achieving their goals. This is a collaborative process; however, it is the client that has to lead the process.

- **Practice through Roleplay:** Harness what is needed regarding physical aspects (body language), communication (the approach to a meeting, words to be used, posture to be adopted, etc.), or engage in roleplay scenarios. This allows individuals to practice and gain experience in the actions necessary to achieve their desired outcomes.

- **Provide Resources:** Follow up a coaching session with, for example, relevant articles, blog posts, book excerpts, or recommended reading for the coaching clients to understand the goal-attainment science and how their actions impact on achieving their goals.

- **Focus on Mindset:** At the follow-up coaching sessions, focus on emotions and mindset. Enable clients to observe changes within themselves. These indicators provide clues for the intelligent questioning route to uncover the "real" issues that move the client forward or create inertia. In this coaching phase, elicit women's sustained focus on the action plan and pursuit of self-correcting behavior that leads them to the outcomes they desire.

- **The Gap Between Goals and Action:** Recognise life is complex. Goal-setting occurs in a vacuum, and action takes place in real-time. Implementing a goal attainment strategy that addresses the potential obstacles women will encounter in pursuing their goals is essential. Any coach worth their salt will take clients through simulated scenarios and enable them to anticipate these hurdles in advance, allowing for better preparation and strategy development. This proactive approach empowers clients to face challenges in their environment with confidence and resilience.

- **Acknowledge the interconnectedness:** Of women with others and systems in coaching. A proficient coach integrates the client's perspective ("I"), relationships ("We"), and systems ("It") in coaching sessions. Visualise this as having two extra chairs for "We" and "It" when the client ("I") joins the coaching

94

process. Effective coaching empowers women to manage "I," "WE," and "IT" perspectives, enhancing goal achievement through self-awareness and dynamic control.

For a successful coaching journey, clients should track their action plans and evaluate their effectiveness. This approach enhances coaching effectiveness and empowers women to take decisive steps towards their goals.

## Phase five: NEW BEGINNINGS

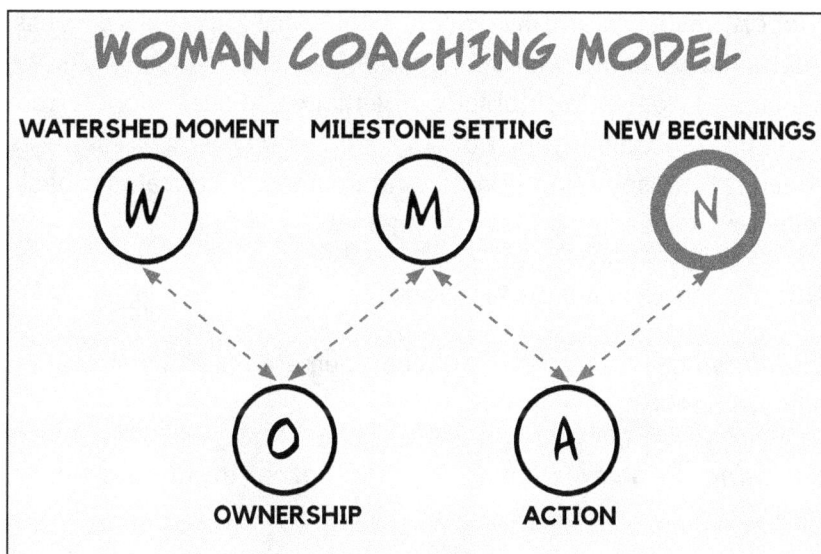

WOMAN COACHING MODEL

WATERSHED MOMENT   MILESTONE SETTING   NEW BEGINNINGS

W   M   N

O   A

OWNERSHIP   ACTION

Without leaping, no amount of learning, preparation, simulation, or insight will yield results. It is often when the client stands at the moment of renewal, reinvention, and restarting of one's life that profound doubt, feelings of unworthiness, and whispers of fear beset them. Although they have completed the watershed phase, reclaimed ownership, set milestones, and pursued actions, the proof of the coaching lies in the client's ability to self-regulate and adopt sustainable behaviour patterns. Therefore, a further coaching phase is necessary: transforming the caterpillar into the butterfly—to embrace the New Beginning!

Women's ability to transition from insight to action and adopt sustainable behaviour patterns propels them from their previous state to inhabit a new persona—the essence of coaching. A critical aspect of this process is that women have developed the insight and skills to self-correct, self-propel, and enact change. The sustainability of action is paramount, and any signs of stagnation or reverting to old behaviours should serve as warning signals.

The new beginnings phase is also about building support systems, and sponsorship and allies are key elements of this. Sponsorship and allies, in the context of coaching, involve active and ongoing support, advocacy, and investment in the coaching client's success. Alternatively stated, "Get your tribe!" This is the stage where we encourage women to embrace authenticity and seek support from a "Shero" tribe comprising both men and women who will serve as cheerleaders, sounding boards, and sources of critical feedback, reflection, validation, and encouragement.

This tribe serves multiple functions:

*Cheerleaders:* Providing encouragement and celebrating achievements, no matter how small.

*Sounding Boards:* Offering a safe space to discuss ideas, challenges, and aspirations.

*Critical Feedback Providers:* Giving honest and constructive feedback to help refine actions and strategies.

*Reflective Mirrors:* Enabling women to see their progress and areas for further development.

*Validators:* Affirming the women's experiences and efforts, reinforcing their sense of worth and capability.

It is also crucial to recognise that in the new beginning phase, moments of relapse or stagnation can also serve as new watershed moments, propelling coaching clients back into the

W-O-M-A-N coaching process. Drawing from my experience as a physiotherapist, I often found that while addressing one issue, such as neck pain, clients would improve, only to reveal a new problem in the process. Similarly, in coaching, the journey of progress often presents new challenges. The circle of life is about forward movement, and encountering new challenges is an inherent part of that progression.

In summary, the new beginnings phase is about moving from preparation to action, ensuring sustainability, and building a robust support system while acknowledging relapses and new challenges are natural parts of the coaching journey.

### *What Women Want Coaches to Know*

Dear Coach,

What a journey it has been! I want to express my heartfelt gratitude for the following:

Thank you for empowering me to move forward confidently. While I am still learning the invaluable lesson of owning both my successes and failures with balance, your coaching has provided me with essential tools for self-reflection, paying attention, and self-correction.

Your constant focus on the way forward is invaluable and makes me feel secure since I know where I am heading. Your emphasis on sustaining my accomplishments inspires me to aim higher in my life. Your efforts in evaluating the options that lie ahead make me determined to reach my envisioned destinations. I appreciate your ability to tap into the hidden part of me that often hesitates to speak boldly about my aspirations.

Your deep listening has allowed me to explore significant goals I wish to attain, and I am eager to delve into these opportunities sooner rather than later.

Reframing my stories has been enlightening. It has enabled me to separate fact from fiction and clarify my narratives.

Thank you for sharing the "streetlight effect" story. Your adaptation of this tale resonated deeply with me. The metaphor of searching for answers where the light is not shining has become my guiding principle, illuminating new pathways to my desired outcomes.

Finally, I deeply appreciate your recognition of the complexity of my experiences.

Deepest appreciation,

Wiser, Happy Woman

## A Guidepost to Coaches

In the new beginning phase, the following pointers can be valuable to coaches:

- **New You, New Challenges:** Recognise that a woman's commitment to new beginnings sometimes leads to new challenges, such as isolation, loneliness, and pushback. We, as coaches, understand the difficulty of presenting oneself as a new you! Therefore, our coaching clients may face efforts to regress to their former selves. Coaches may need to offer ongoing support in navigating these challenges and scheduling regular check-ins. During this phase, remind the coaching client to engage with the "Shero tribes."

- **The Cycle of Action and Reflection:** The new beginning phase is a dynamic period characterised by both action and reflection.

It's a time when clients take proactive steps towards their goals while also reflecting on their progress and adjusting their plans as necessary. This phase is not reactive but responsive to any changes and circumstances.

- **Tools for Resilience:** Provide women with coaching tools to monitor, recognise, and respond to relapses of old behaviours that could lead to setbacks. Continue encouraging the process of reflection and maintaining the courage to pursue different approaches to achieve the outcome they are striving for. Emphasise flexibility and adaptability are key to propelling them toward their goals.

- **New Beginnings and Endings:** Ending the coaching relationship is as essential as the contracting phase. Coaching cannot be infinite; we contract with our clients for a specific number of sessions. At the end of these sessions, we conduct an evaluation. However, if necessary, the client could request additional coaching, and then we would renew the contract.

- **Evaluate the Completed Coaching Engagement:** The new beginnings phase is a time for both the client and the coach to also evaluate the entire coaching journey. This evaluation focuses on the achievements, challenges, and areas for further development. Encourage your client to provide feedback on the coaching process. What aspects were most helpful? What could be improved? This feedback will not only support their continued development but also strengthen your coaching practices.

- **Embrace New Beginnings:** Acknowledge that all endings signify new beginnings, opening doors for new opportunities and continued development.

The new beginnings phase is a transformative time for the client and the coach. By thoroughly evaluating the coaching journey, offering ongoing coaching support to navigate new challenges, balancing action with reflection, and equipping women with resilience-building tools, coaches can ensure women transition confidently into their new way of being in the world and navigating the world, ready to face future challenges with self-assurance.

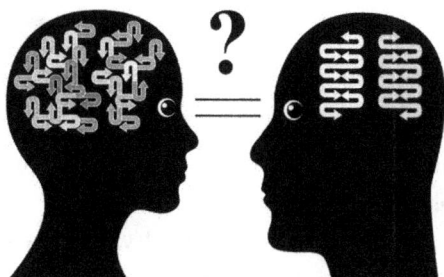

## CHAPTER 5

# MAPPING THE GENDER-INTELLIGENT COACHING FRAMEWORK

*Synthesis is about understanding the whole and the parts at the same time, along with the relationships and the connections that make up the dynamics of the whole.*

Leyla Acaroglu
(Designer, Sociologist, Circular Provocateur)

Contemplating what to include in this book, this chapter hovered on the brink of exclusion. I pondered whether delving into the theoretical foundations of the gender-intelligent coaching approach might be redundant, given the available published works on these theories. However, discussions with my coaching tribe yielded a consensus. This chapter should go beyond merely disseminating theories; it should reveal the reasoning behind adopting these theories that shape the gender-intelligent coaching approach.

Moreover, in the spirit of engagement underpinning this book, it offers you as coaches an opportunity to reflect on the theories you have adopted into your coaching practice and perhaps consider integrating additional ones.

In chapter three, I drew a symbolic parallel between the coaching framework and the pylons of a bridge, highlighting that the pylons hold the bridge in place and the coaching framework plays an essential role in supporting the coaching intervention. This chapter demonstrates how I've intertwined various theoretical strands—such as gender theory, James Flaherty's integral coaching, Seiler's ontological coaching, Ken Wilber's integral theory, social psychology, motivational and goal attainment theory, and neuroscience—to develop a comprehensive and adaptable coaching intervention. Through my coaching practice, I've witnessed the effectiveness of the gender-intelligent coaching framework in addressing a wide array of coaching issues and diverse gender-related challenges faced by women coaching clients. However, it's important to note that this book only provides a brief overview of the theories supporting the gender-intelligent coaching approach.

For a deeper exploration, I recommend delving into the works of esteemed theorists like Judith Butler, Dorothy Black, Simone de Beauvoir, and Bell Hooks for gender theory, and literature on Flaherty's integral coaching, Seiler's ontological coaching, and Wilber's integral theory. Additionally, insights from neuroscience research by experts such as Amy Cuddy, David Rock, and Tara Swart, along with the works of theorists like Albert Bandura, John Whitmore, Angela Duckworth, and James Clear on motivation and goal attainment theory, can further enrich your understanding. While this list is not exhaustive, it provides a starting point for engaging with thought leaders' works to enhance your coaching practice and make a greater impact.

These theories are, of course, not the only theories that inform my coaching approach. Therefore, the gender-intelligent coaching approach framework is always ready to integrate new theories. As coaches committed to unleashing human potential, it is paramount to nurture a mindset of continual curiosity. Yes, curiosity—that concept again! This insistence on practising curiosity stems from my belief that maintaining an inquisitive stance enables us to uncover solutions to both our challenges and those of our clients. Thus, whenever I encounter empirical theories that could benefit my clients and myself on our transformational journey, I integrate them seamlessly into the gender-intelligent coaching approach.

So, without further delay, let's summarise the theoretical foundations of the gender-intelligent coaching approach, along with the rationale for intertwining these theories into the gender-intelligent coaching framework.

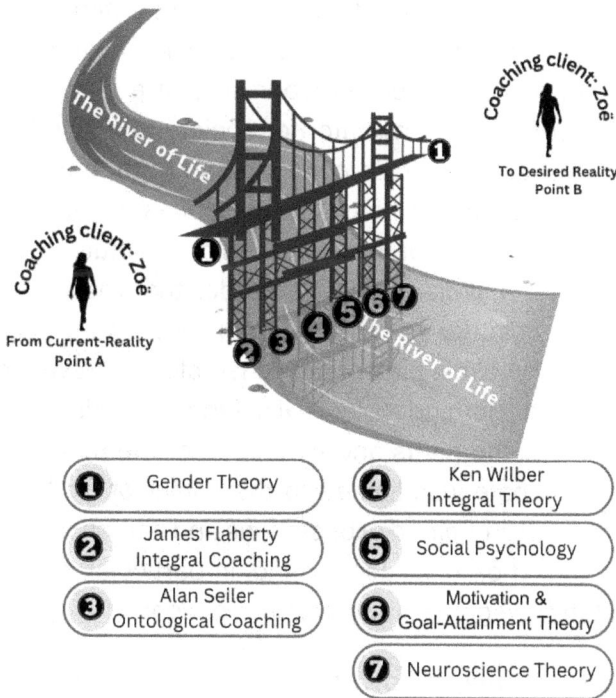

*Figure 8: The Theoretical Underpinnings of the Gender-Intelligent Coaching Framework*

# GENDER THEORY - It is a Boy! It is a Girl!

In the gender-intelligent coaching framework, theories on gender serve as the critical horizontal and foundational pillar, anchoring all other theories incorporated in developing the gender-intelligent coaching approach.

In gender theory, we explore the intricate web of cultural expectations and biases that shape our perceptions of masculinity and femininity[85]. Before delving into these complex waters, it is essential to grasp key concepts such as sex and gender.

First, "sex" refers to a person's biological sex, specifically the X and Y chromosomes, which determine the biological markers that identify a baby as a boy or girl. Second, we have "gender," which denotes the societal construction of roles associated with being a girl, boy, man, or woman within a specific society. Gender theorists emphasise that it is crucial to recognise that a child's biological sex merely serves as an indicator for society to shape the child's behaviour, appearance, dress code, and so forth, based on what society perceives as feminine and masculine. Gender theorists urge us to grasp that our biology shouldn't dictate our destiny, as it often does in society today. Consider the classic illustration of babies and colours: At birth, you pop out, and suddenly, the world decides if you're a pink or blue character. However, the issue extends beyond clothing colour—it's fundamentally about who chooses to wear the pants and who opts for the pink frilly dress. We wish the debate was limited to the colour of clothes; but its about the deeper, ingrained expectations and limitations placed on individuals based on their gender and, in particular, the profound and devastating negative impact it has on women.

At the heart of the gender theory lies the power difference associated with being born female or male. A patriarchal society assigns more power and privilege to men while marginalising women. In other words, in patriarchal societies, men get the golden

104

ticket: they are granted more power, more privilege, more authority, the corner office, and a voice at the table. Women? Not so much. Although both men and women are then boxed into stereotypical roles, it is women who draw the short end of the stick since they are saddled with negative stereotypical portrayals such as women being "too emotional" or too soft for leadership roles in contrast with the perception of men being "rational" leaders. Even though these stereotypes have been debunked through solid empirical studies, they are enduring, and as the evidence corroborates, they can impact everything from who gets hired for specific jobs to who gets listened to and who deserves power[86].

Critically, gender theorists delve into the profound negative impact power imbalances and power dynamics have on women. Consequently, they challenge societal stereotypes about men and women and advocate for reshaping gender norms to foster a gender-equitable society that allows women to thrive. This involves recognising the oppressive nature of gendered expectations and constructions and then working to dismantle systems that perpetuate oppression and discrimination.

Furthermore, gender theorists emphasise that gender intersects with other dimensions of our identity, such as race, class, and sexuality, which can lead to compounding forms of discrimination and oppression. For instance, individuals who identify as female, belong to marginalised racial groups and occupy lower socioeconomic statuses face compounded forms of discrimination.

In summary, gender is not an immutable biological determinant but rather a socially constructed framework. Advancing gender equity necessitates dismantling systems that sustain and perpetuate male privilege and inhibit the full realisation of women's potential based solely on their assigned sex at birth. This calls for a critical examination of entrenched gender norms and a commitment to fostering an inclusive society where all individuals can thrive, regardless of gender.

## Amalgamating Gender Theory and the Gender Intelligent Coaching Approach

The gender-intelligent coaching approach incorporates theories of gender into our coaching practices since it acknowledges that patriarchal norms continue to pose a formidable challenge to women and their social advancement. Furthermore, by integrating gender theory, we allow women coaching clients to gain a deeper understanding of how gender shapes their individual experiences, behaviours, expectations, and progress. Having a critical awareness of how gender impacts women will undoubtedly mean coaches do not fall into the following positions: succumbing to denialism by ignoring individuals' social contexts or conformism by suggesting that other social views are superior or siding with the dominant social view.

Instead, the gender-intelligent coaching approach recommends mainstreaming gender theory in the coaching approach. Through this action, coaches demonstrate respect for the client's context, equip clients with skills to engage critically with their context, and clients take ownership and proactive action to mitigate the negative impact of gender bias on their lives. This approach validates clients' gendered experiences and offers a safe space for exploring and challenging societal pressures and expectations.

For example, in some, if not most nations, the prevailing gender script dictates that a woman's main role is to be a carer, and having a professional career is a choice but not an essential part of her identity. A gender-intelligent coaching approach empowers clients to navigate these gendered challenges by questioning gender prescripts and contesting stereotypes. By understanding how societal expectations shape individuals' experiences and behaviours, coaches can assist coaching clients in developing personalised strategies that account for the intersectionality of gender with other social identities such as race, class, sexual orientation, disability, and ethnicity. This approach validates clients' gendered experiences and provides a safe space for exploring and challenging societal pressures and expectations.

Many women coaching clients grapple with balancing numerous roles and responsibilities, often while their partners have the luxury of prioritising career growth over childcare and household functions. Even when male partners share caregiving duties, their contributions may be considered optional rather than essential. For instance, I coached a woman who was the director of a large non-profit organisation. She felt overwhelmed by the demands of leading her organisation while also managing her household and caring for her four children, all under the age of eighteen. Through multiple coaching sessions, she realised the necessity of reorganising household and caregiving responsibilities. Although she initially indicated she would never gain buy-in from her spouse for sharing household tasks, she found him willing to assist with childcare responsibilities. His cooperation in sharing childcare tasks surprised her since she had assumed he would not do it. Recognising the imbalance in household responsibilities and how time-consuming they are, she made strategic decisions to optimise her time. She chose to hire a domestic worker two days a week to delegate some cleaning tasks, allowing her to carve out quality time for herself and her children during moments of respite. This case highlights the importance of acknowledging women's social context, enabling the woman coaching client to take charge of her life and, in this case, her time management, despite the influence of entrenched gender norms.

In another coaching session, I worked with a woman manager who operated in a male-dominated office environment. Despite her competence, she frequently felt overlooked or dismissed during meetings compared to her male counterparts, and she also started to doubt whether she had the skills to compete in such an environment. Research indicating the systematic undervaluation of women's contributions in such settings validated her experiences, and the coaching facilitated a transformation in her perception of her situation. Through coaching, she developed enhanced self-efficacy and strategies to express her contribution with confidence and assertiveness. By altering her approach, she effectively commanded the same level of consideration as her male colleagues without explicitly addressing sexism or gender biases. This case exemplifies how coaching can empower individuals to navigate gender dynamics in the workplace and achieve professional success. Overall, a gender-intelligent coaching intervention enriches the coaching process by fostering greater awareness of how gender dynamics and gender bias impact one's life. Or, to put it another way, you know where the crocodiles swim and have developed a strategy to cross the river safely.

Coaches create transformative experiences through gender-intelligent coaching that empower clients to excel both personally and professionally. Furthermore, through the gender-intelligent approach, they could emerge as advocates for gender equality and promote positive societal change within their communities, organisations, and society.

In conclusion, integrating gender theory into the gender-intelligent coaching approach represents a pivotal step in addressing the pervasive challenges posed by patriarchal norms and advancing gender equality. By deepening our understanding of how gender shapes individual experiences, behaviours, and expectations, we equip coaches and clients with the tools to navigate societal pressures and biases effectively. Through this approach, we validate our clients' gendered experiences and create a supportive environment for exploration and growth. The transformative nature of the gender-intelligent coaching approach empowers clients to excel personally and professionally while fostering advocacy for gender equality and empowering women to achieve their full potential.

# JAMES FLAHERTY'S INTEGRAL COACHING APPROACH

Enter the world of James Flaherty's integral coaching approach—a transformative coaching approach that first captured my attention way back in 2005. While coaching and goal-achievement are often mentioned in one breath, Flaherty believes coaching can serve a nobler cause than only being a goal-driven profession. He advocates expanding the goal of coaching to coach our clients towards achieving holistic personal and professional growth by facilitating fundamental transformational shifts in beliefs, perspectives, and values. For instance, what is the point of coaching a CEO to increase her productivity if, after attaining her productivity goals, the CEO remains arrogant, has narcissistic tendencies and is unable to inspire her staff? Therefore, Flaherty's approach resonated with me strongly because it challenges the notion that success is solely defined by external accomplishments, emphasising the importance of inner transformation alongside external accomplishments and becoming a better, more authentic version of oneself.

Furthermore, he posits that the coaching process is designed to improve the client's ability to self-correct—to change behaviour—when there are disparities between their desired outcomes and actual results, as well as when there is a discrepancy between the values they purport to hold and their performative behaviours. Importantly, Flaherty's integral coaching proposes that an essential part of our transformation is our ability to engage in self-generated behaviours supporting long-term competence. Now, that was quite a mouthful!

My question was: How does Flaherty's integral approach train for long-term competence, self-correction, and self-generation? Flaherty emphasises the impact our clients' interpretations of events have on their actions and mentality. But how does a coach assess a client's interpretation of the world? Flaherty has you covered there as well. He addresses this through his coaching methodology, guiding coaches to consider a client's mood, language, and body. Whoa! The body, language, and mood? Are we still speaking coaching? One of the most compelling aspects of Flaherty's integral coaching approach is its holistic nature. Unlike traditional coaching models that focus predominantly on specific goals or competencies, his integral coaching integrates aspects of body, mind, emotions, and spirit, recognising true transformation requires addressing the whole person. The often-overlooked significance of the body in coaching is emphasised by Flaherty's integral coaching approach, which asserts that our physical state greatly influences our actions, perceptions of possibility, and even our interpersonal interactions.

In contrast to most coaching approaches, which omit focusing on the body, Flaherty's emphasis on the body holds particular importance for the gender-intelligent coaching approach. Historically, the working world has severed the relationship between the mind and the body, treating the latter as a mere vehicle to transport us from point A to point B. However, ignoring the body and its messages denies us valuable information and insights into our thoughts, emotions, responses, behaviour, and overall well-being.

He argues that our language reveals our assumptions, beliefs, and values. By providing new language, coaches can assist clients in reshaping their perspectives and opening up new possibilities for action. For instance, a client who habitually uses language that reflects helplessness ("I can't") can be guided to adopt more empowering language ("I will find a way"). This shift changes how the client talks about their situation and thinks and feels about it.

Next, we consider the client's primary mood. It is widely known our dominant mood shapes how we interact with the world and affects our decision-making. For instance, feeling resigned may create a sense of powerlessness and the belief that change is unattainable. Conversely, a mood of ambition can unlock various opportunities and motivate goal attainment.

Importantly, Flaherty urges coaches to consider that each coaching client is at a different stage of development and competence, and we need to take this into account when working with human beings. He says this in the context of cautioning coaches wanting to use a one-size-fits-all methodology to coach all clients as if they are all the same. Like me, you probably want to know how to measure your clients' level of development. Again, Flaherty's got you covered, and he proposes various development assessments coaches can use to assess clients' levels or stages of development in a particular domain. I find this aspect very useful when working with clients since, in the process of doing their assessments, they also gain insight into where they are at and which areas they still need to grow in.

Finally, the cherry on top, and the clincher for incorporating Flaherty in the gender-intelligent coaching framework was that he advocates for a particular relationship between the client and coach; he calls for the coaching relationship to be a symbiotic relationship, where both the coach and clients continue to learn and grow in the coaching partnership. This is an undervalued differentiator between coaching and other human-care professions. In coaching, we walk with our clients and do not regard ourselves as the genie with the answers. In other words, we are equal to our clients; there is no inferior or superior caste language.

## Why Integrate Flaherty's Integral Coaching Approach?

Integrating Flaherty's integral coaching was a critical step in developing the gender-intelligent coaching framework. Flaherty's integral theory emphasises understanding clients in their entirety—considering their physical, emotional, mental, and spiritual dimensions. This holistic perspective is crucial for gender-intelligent coaching, where gender-specific experiences and challenges are often profoundly interconnected with various aspects of a person's life. For instance, women might face unique stressors related to balancing professional responsibilities and family care, impacting their physical health, emotional well-being, and self-perception.

The emphasis on shifting our interpretation of the world by reflecting on our language, developing an awareness of our body, and understanding our mood could be critical to changing how we engage with the world around us. Given we live in a gendered world, by incorporating Flaherty's integral coaching, our women coaching clients can gain insight into their interpretation of the gendered world they inhabit and develop a linguistic capability to explain their experiences with gender bias and discrimination.

Similarly, addressing the body's role, such as the impact of stress or societal expectations on physical well-being, can enable clients in developing healthier habits and greater resilience. Understanding and working with clients' moods can also help coach them to navigate and overcome gender-specific emotional challenges, such as impostor syndrome or burnout.

The gender-intelligent coaching approach similarly encourages women to pay attention to their physical well-being because it provides critical insights into their state of being. The gender-intelligent coaching approach explicitly observes the body's response to discrimination, undermining, or threats. For example, being aware of their bodies' signals allows women to engage with difficult emotions, empowering them to respond confidently. For instance, if they enter meetings feeling alienated or anxious, by simply being aware that their bodies are on alert and tense, allows them to pursue practices to calm and ground their emotions.

Importantly, women's language can be empowering or disempowering in creating their desired world. For example, when coaching women clients, I often focus on drawing their attention to the language they use to describe themselves. For example, women often use self-deprecating language in self-descriptions. They seldom use terms such as "I am an authoritative voice," "an expert," or "a specialist," and when introducing themselves, they often downplay their achievements.

And, of course, the clincher to include Flaherty's integral coaching was that in the gender-intelligent coaching approach, our coaching clients presume ownership of the coaching journey, and we do not perpetuate the inferior-superior dynamics.

# ONTOLOGICAL COACHING

I came across James Flaherty's integral coaching approach and Alan Seiler's ontological coaching approach, more or less at the same time. Alan Seiler is regarded as the founder of ontological coaching, and again, my recommendation is, whether you are an ontological coach or not, it is worthy of your coaching practice to gain insight into Alan Seiler's ontological coaching approach.

The etymology of the word "ontos" means *being*. Thus, the philosophical, existential inquiry into the nature of being and how individuals construct their reality, show up and behave in the world form the foundation of ontological coaching. Ontology refers to our presence in the world as our "way of being". Like the integral coaching approach, ontological coaching emphasises the importance of the body, language, and emotions. Ontological coaching encourages clients to explore their "way of being" and uncover underlying patterns of thinking, feeling, and acting that may limit their potential.

The outcome ontological coaching strives to achieve is for coaching clients to gain a profound insight into their way of being and also understand what informs their way of being and how their interpretation of events informs their behaviour. For instance, a woman coaching client reported she usually gets angry with her supervisor when she receives critical feedback. The inability to remain calm and appreciate feedback, even when negative, will likely impact her career advancement prospects. What perhaps might seem to be a problem in her work context soon revealed this is her way of being—angry and defensive when receiving negative feedback whether from her supervisor or from family and friends. In ontological coaching, we say her "way of being" when she receives critical feedback is a fight response. Until the client gains insight into how she shows up in the world she will continue apportioning blame to her supervisor and identify her as the problem.

## Integrating Seiler's Ontological Coaching Approach

Two factors motivated me to include ontological coaching concepts in the gender-intelligent coaching framework. Similar to Flaherty's integral coaching, ontological coaching focuses on how we verbalise our experiences and how our words create our reality and thus our world—and like Flaherty, Seiler posits that how we use language and communicate influences how we view and interact with the world around us and the response we receive from the world.

By changing our language and interpretation, we can change how we view our lives and the world around us. We express our way of being through three domains: language, emotions, and physiology (body). Impressive, hey! For coaches, it means we focus on the way the client communicates, the language they use, their emotions, and their physiological expression.

The other aspect of Seiler's coaching approach that resonates with me, because it mirrors one of my coaching values, is that human beings often seek answers to their life dilemmas by expecting the solution to be external to them. However, frequently the answers we seek to our life dilemmas are within us. Not in the sense of "Oh, I know everything already and do not have to rely on anyone." Instead, with the right coaching questions, the clients can unearth strategies from within themselves to address their life challenges. This process of self-discovery and finding solutions, facilitated by coaching, inevitably leads to developing actionable strategies to achieve their goals. Gender-intelligent coaching, then, is about coaching clients to gain insight into the fact that they hold the resolutions to the challenges they face. It empowers them to tap into their own potential, uncover new possibilities, and develop strategies to overcome their obstacles. The essence of this approach is not just in finding solutions but in recognising and harnessing the innate ability of our clients to navigate and conquer their challenges.

Consider this case study: a coaching client, let's call her Thandeka, consistently leaned towards a negative self-assessment of herself. She was on the verge of giving up on her overdue PhD. In our first coaching session, she repeatedly referred to the PhD journey as, "I'm battling my PhD". Utilising the ontological coaching approach, we focused on the language she used, specifically the word "battle," and explored why she referred to the PhD journey in this way. She expressed she felt as though she was engaged in a kind of tug-of-war with her PhD, one where she was often defeated. She explained she would often sit in front of her computer, ready to work on her PhD, but then feel so overwhelmed that she would give up. Not surprisingly, she suffered from anxiety, stress, and procrastination, which consequently led to her failure to meet her PhD milestones. Applying the ontological coaching approach and using the coaching tool of generative and incisive coaching questions, we explored the language of framing her PhD as her "battle." Thandeka gained insight that the very idea of framing it as "battling with my PhD" triggered immediate anxiety, putting her body in flight mode, which in turn caused chronic procrastination. Reframing the word from "battle" to the concept of "exploration" opened a new way for her to approach the journey of completing her PhD. From then on, she no longer saw it as a battle to work on her PhD thesis but rather embraced the mindset of being on a journey to capture her thoughts by working on her PhD.

To summarise, ontological coaching is a comprehensive coaching approach that underscores our nature as mean-making machines—by constantly creating our reality through the stories we tell ourselves[87]. By understanding and shifting these narratives, individuals can transform their beliefs and behaviours to achieve their desired outcomes. This approach emphasises the importance of language, emotions, and physical state in shaping our perception of reality, ultimately influencing our actions and results. By addressing these elements, ontological coaching offers a framework for personal growth and transformation.

# KEN WILBER'S INTEGRAL THEORY

I delved into Wilber's integral theory, motivated both by the necessity of fulfilling a requirement of the master's degree and by realising it was the same, Wilber who wrote the book that was so impactful in my life journey, i.e. "Grace and Grit". This book profoundly moved me years prior, long before I considered pursuing coaching[88]. The book chronicled the poignant journey of a husband and wife who faced a cancer diagnosis, their journey with cancer and eventually the wife's passing. To my surprise, the author of that impactful book was none other than Ken Wilber. What a coincidence!

Initially delving into Wilber's integral theory, I found myself stuck in Wilber's integral theory sauna, so to speak, and mentally sweated for weeks trying to figure out what all the fuss was about. However, as I learned more about his integral philosophy, I came to understand that Wilber sought to integrate all known knowledge or truths about human development from various philosophies, religions, psychology, and sciences into one coherent framework, which he called AQAL (All Quadrants, All Lines). No wonder he needed to go on a three-year retreat! In the interest of saving the forest, I must insist you read his offerings. But I warn you, it is not easy reading. Or perhaps you bright sparks will find it easy.

Wilber's four-quadrant model is the pièce de résistance of his integral philosophy and provided me with the best entry point to shed light on his integral approach to human experience and knowledge. Let's just say Wilber had me when he said, "four-quadrant model".

The four-quadrant model is a very neat conceptual way to understand the human experience and examine any given phenomenon, knowledge, and event from four perspectives. The main objective of the four-quadrant model is to gain a holistic understanding of said phenomenon. Have I lost you here? Let me explain further.

The model essentially breaks down human experience into four dimensions: individual interior, individual exterior, collective interior, and collective exterior. By examining a phenomenon from all four perspectives, you can gain a more comprehensive understanding of it. This holistic approach allows for a deeper analysis and appreciation of the complexities of the human experience. These quadrants are named I, IT, WE, and ITS, or Individual Subjective, Individual Objective, Interior Collective, and Exterior Collective. The I, IT, WE, and ITS quadrants provide a framework for analysing various aspects of human experience from different angles.

This paradigm aids in the discovery of deeper insights and connections that might otherwise go unnoticed when seeing only one perspective.

| INTERIOR INDIVIDUAL SUBJECTIVE | EXTERIOR INDIVIDUAL OBJECTIVE |
|---|---|
| I | IT |
| Thoughts, Emotions, Beliefs, Values and Aspirations | Body, Biology, Physical and Social |
| INTERIOR COLLECTIVE | EXTERIOR COLLECTIVE |
| WE | ITS |
| Culture, Worldviews, Relationships, Language | Organisational Systems, Structures and Policies |

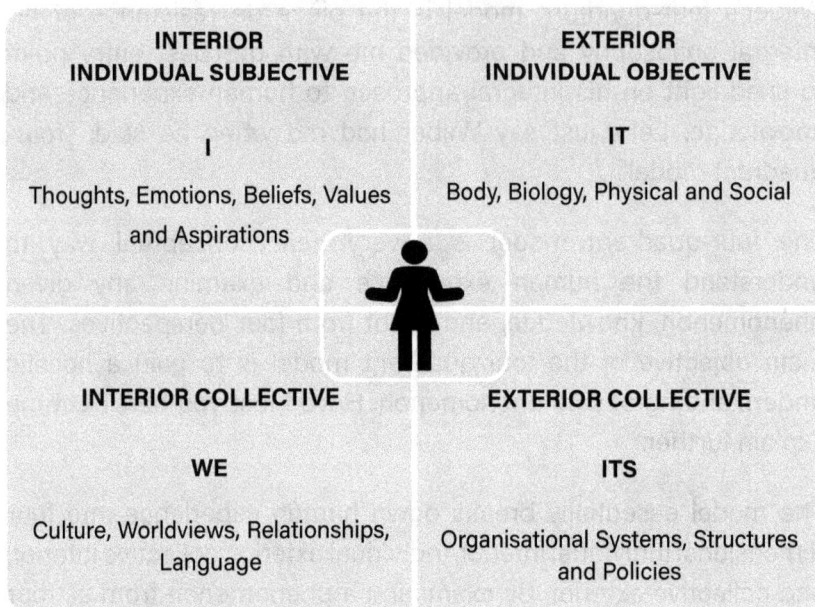

*Figure 10: Ken Wilber's four quadrant model*

The upper left (UL), the "I" or "Individual Subjective" domain, focuses purely on the individual's subjective experiences—one's emotions, opinions, thoughts, dreams, etc.

The upper right (UR) quadrant, the "IT" or "Individual Objective" domain, is where the elements of what is happening to the person can be measured and observed. For example, when you put someone in magnetic resonance imaging, you can see which part of the brain lights up when the person has a certain thought. A heart rate monitor can measure the heart rate increases or decreases, allowing you to measure the physiological state of the person, the breathing rate, and so forth.

The "I" and "IT" quadrants are focused on the individual mind-body system. However, to make sense of the mind-body system, we must also take into consideration the environment in which the person is located. The lower left (LL) quadrant, which is the "WE" or "Interior Collective" domain, poses the most challenging to grasp because it encompasses culture, language, value systems, and worldview of a group, the collective, and the community.

The fourth piece of the puzzle is the lower right "ITS" or "Exterior Collective" Quadrant, which represents the empirical side of collective reality. For example, the systemic factors, such as demography, technology, and structures, that impact individuals.

The essence of Wilber's integral theory posits that humans exist within all four domains, and by comprehensively examining the human experience and development through each of these perspectives, we can achieve a holistic understanding of the world around us, since we have a comprehensive framework for understanding the complexities of life.

## Merging Wilber's Theory into the Gender-Intelligent Coaching Framework

There are no rewards for guessing why I included Ken's Wilber theory in the gender-intelligent coaching approach. When we coach women using the four-quadrant model, we gift them this holistic template to navigate their experiences from various angles or quadrants, which in turn allows them to consider the interface between internal experiences, external factors, and collective influences that shape their experiences. By incorporating Ken Wilber's theory into the gender-intelligent coaching approach, we coach to provide a comprehensive framework that allows women to gain insight into the interconnectedness of their inner world with the external world. This holistic perspective enables a deeper exploration of personal growth and development in a more integrated way.

Furthermore, the four-quadrant model provides a powerful tool for coaches and coaching clients to gain a deeper understanding of the complexities of their experiences. By focusing on external factors influencing women's personal growth, coaches can tailor their approach to address all aspects of their clients' lives. This integrated method can lead to more effective and sustainable results in the coaching process.

In summary, Ken Wilber's integral theory enhances the gender-intelligent coaching approach by providing a comprehensive, multidimensional framework that fosters deeper understanding and more effective coaching interventions. This integration not only enriches the coaching process but also empowers women to achieve personal and professional growth more holistically and sustainably.

# SOCIAL PSYCHOLOGY

Social psychology explores how group settings influence individual thoughts, emotions, and behaviours. This field sheds light on concepts such as social influence, social conformity, group dynamics, and group cohesion[89]. This includes both direct influence, such as persuasion and peer pressure, and indirect influence, like societal norms and cultural expectations. Social conformity, a subset of social influence, highlights how individuals often adjust their behaviours or attitudes to align with the group norm.

Social psychologists assert that our surroundings, contexts, and interpersonal interactions profoundly influence us, challenging the common assumption of autonomous self-determination in personal decision-making and interpretation of events.

## The Fusion of Social Psychology into the Gender-Intelligent Coaching Framework

Incorporating social psychology into my gender-sensitive coaching approach was an obvious choice because, as a coach, I deal firsthand with how social environments and group interactions can influence cognitive functions and behaviours.

Take one of my clients, for example. The presenting coaching issue was that she was experiencing an existential crisis regarding her work commitment and maternal responsibilities in childcare. Instead of diving into her turmoil head-on, the coaching focused on her social context. While her work offered an encouraging "you go, gal!" vibe, as soon as she entered her abode on her return from work, her mother (who lives with her) reminded her about parental duties. For example, her mother would say, "When a child comes home from school, he needs his mother to speak to and a plate of home-cooked food". The role of coaching wasn't to dictate, but to illuminate how her social context and her mother's opinion were shaping her opinion. During the coaching intervention, the client relinquished self-imposed guilt and reframed her maternal role, recognising the legitimacy of her distinct caregiving approach compared to her mother's paradigm.

Cultivating profound self-insight lies at the core of coaching and the gender-intelligent coaching approach. Integrating social psychology offers invaluable insights for our coaching clients to understand how social norms influence their emotions, beliefs, and behaviours, especially regarding gender roles and norms. Women often face multifaceted decisions influenced by societal expectations and pressures, whether in career pursuits or traditional gender roles. As coaches, our role is to provide a pedagogical tool enabling them to grasp the factors affecting their emotions, decisions, and behaviour. Equipped with this cognitive tool, coaching recipients can navigate prevalent stereotypes, making well-informed decisions aligned with their innate aspirations and ambitions.

In conclusion, integrating social psychology into the gender-intelligent coaching framework significantly enhances the coaching process by providing a deeper understanding of how social contexts and group dynamics influence individual behaviour. By acknowledging and addressing these social influences, coaches can enable clients to uncover the underlying factors shaping their thoughts, emotions, and actions. This comprehensive approach empowers clients to make informed, authentic decisions that align with their true aspirations, free from the constraints of societal expectations.

# MOTIVATIONAL AND GOAL-ATTAINMENT THEORY

Motivational and goal-attainment theories focus on the psychological factors that influence goal achievement. While some theorists contend that people have an innate desire to reach their full potential, others hold that rewards and unfavourable outcomes play a significant role in motivating behaviour. Ultimately, understanding the interplay between internal drives and external influences can provide valuable insights into how individuals can effectively set and achieve their goals. However, there is no doubt, backed up by research, that whether goals are intrinsically motivated or externally driven, those who set goals are more successful than non-goal setters. This is because the act of goal-setting is crucial as it directs focus and effort towards what needs to be accomplished[90].

Goal-attainment is fundamental to the coaching industry. In fact, I refer to coaches as goal-attainment gurus, since central to most training programmes in coaching, is the focus on goal-attainment and motivational theories. Therefore, I think any coach who is worth their salt ought to be knowledgeable in motivational theory and the science of goal-attainment, at the very minimum.

To direct the goal coaching intervention, the gender-intelligent coaching framework leans on theories of self-determination and self-efficacy. Self-determination theory (SDT) emphasises the fundamental psychological requirements which govern human motivation and action[91]. According to SDT, people have an innate inclination towards development, autonomy, and integration, yet this is dependent on the social context in which they find themselves. According to the theory, social settings can either enhance or undermine people's intrinsic motivational drive. Individuals are more likely to evolve and integrate psychologically when their social environments promote autonomy, competence, and connectedness. In contrast, circumstances that limit autonomy, undercut competence or lack supportive connections can hamper people's determination, resulting in poor self-actualisation.

Another factor that influences goal accomplishment is whether you believe you can accomplish the goal you have set for yourself. This belief is called self-efficacy. Self-efficacy is defined as confidence in one's capacity to successfully perform specific tasks effectively in order to achieve or realise one's goals[92].

Although conviction or trust in one's talents typically results in constructive action, doubting one's abilities often leads to failure or passivity. Self-efficacy beliefs are built from both direct and indirect experiences, social evaluations from others, and one's psychological, physiological, and emotional state during task accomplishment.

## Weaving the Goal-Attainment Theories and Motivational Theories into the fabric of the Gender-Intelligent Coaching Framework

By weaving goal-attainment theories and motivational theories into the gender-intelligent coaching framework, we address a critical issue: the gendered nature of ambition and motivation. Critics have long claimed that women fall behind in leadership positions due to their reportedly lesser desire and increased aversion to risk. However, the research tells a different story: societal biases and stereotypes cast a pall over women's agency and autonomy, impeding their pursuit of goals. The gender-intelligent coaching framework maintains that women have an equal capability for goal achievement and motivation as men, but the uneven social landscape significantly skews the playing field. Crucially, studies reveal a common feature between men and women: both have ambitious objectives, but women also embrace goals with prosocial motivations.

Although research reflects both men and women run the same goal attainment race and are equally motivated, women encounter curveballs, potholes, and differentiated levels of encouragement. Society shapes women to view themselves not just as differently abled but *less* abled, which impacts women's psyche. Not surprisingly, research shows women have lower self-efficacy, self-esteem, and higher levels of self-doubt and insecurity[93].

In essence, integrating self-determination and self-efficacy theories into the gender-intelligent coaching framework is of paramount significance in coaching women. These theories not only clarify the intricacies of motivation but also guide the coaching intervention to promote self-efficacy in women, thus ensuring women achieve their targeted goals.

# THE NEUROSCIENCES THEORY

One of the most ground-breaking advancements in coaching interventions has been the integration of neuroscience into coaching practice. The scientific study of the nervous system and brain, known as neuroscience, provides coaches with unparalleled insights into the intricate workings of the human mind.

Neuroplasticity, or the brain's capacity to rewire, remodel and adapt, is one of the critical concepts in neuroscience that holds enormous promise for coaching. By understanding how the brain can rewire itself through neuroplasticity, coaches can aid clients to break free from limiting beliefs and developing new habits that align with their desired outcomes[94].

The two neuroscience-based concepts I felt would be empowering for women and thus incorporated into the gender-intelligent coaching framework, are Amy Cuddy's power pose and David Rock's SCARF methodology.

# Cuddy's Power Poses

Social psychologist Amy Cuddy introduced the concept of "power poses," which is specific body postures believed to influence both our mental state and how we are perceived by others[95]. This resonated with the gender-intelligent coaching approach because power poses emphasise the strong connection between an individual's body and mind, as our body reflects our mental state.

According to Cuddy, "power poses" such as an expansive body posture (a high-power pose), like standing tall, shoulders back, legs spread apart, or with hands on the hips or arms wide open, convey feelings of control, confidence, and power[96]. In contrast, low-power poses or contractive body posture—slumping, crossed legs, and arms. Research suggests that adopting these power poses can trigger hormonal changes in the body, leading to an increase in testosterone, a hormone associated with confidence, and a decrease in cortisol, a hormone associated with stress[97]. Cuddy's findings offer valuable insights into how our body language can enhance our confidence, presence, and how others perceive us.

### Including Cuddy's Power Pose into the gender-intelligent coaching framework

Yes, how cool is that? The way we position our bodies can impact the results of our actions and the way others perceive us. Since discovering Cuddy's power pose thesis, I have incorporated it into my coaching interventions, particularly for women coaching clients who struggle with internal doubts, confidence issues, and workplace environments where biases and stereotypes limit them. This simple yet powerful technique has often led to enhanced authority and confidence in my clients, empowering them to confront their challenges head-on.

Again, there are no rewards for guessing why I would use Cuddy's power pose as part of the gender-intelligent coaching arsenal. Gender dynamics and societal expectations often place women in positions of perceived powerlessness or subordination. Consequently, women face unique challenges when asserting themselves confidently and breaking through barriers. The power pose technique provides a practical tool to enhance women's confidence and influence, enabling them to navigate and overcome these obstacles more easily. Moreover, by adopting the power pose, women can tap into and connect with their personal power, which is especially valuable in situations where women may feel marginalised or undervalued.

The power pose can equip women with valuable tools to counteract the effects of gender bias. By adopting powerful postures, women can project confidence and authority that challenge societal stereotypes and promotes equal treatment.

Gender-intelligent coaches can coach women to integrate the power pose into their lives and build solid self-confidence foundations.

Leadership positions often require a commanding presence and the ability to inspire and influence others. When women deal with a host of barriers, biases, and discrimination, the power pose can be a tool to aid them in cultivating a leadership presence that embodies strength, confidence, and gravitas. This can empower women to navigate leadership challenges effectively and assert their authority in a way that aligns with their authentic selves.

## David Rock's SCARF model

Drawing from neuroscience, David Rock provides insight into how the brain responds to social stimuli[98]. Rock states that the human brain is a social organ and wired for social connections.

Thus, our interaction with others profoundly influences not only emotions but also physiological and neurological reactions[99]. According to Rock's research, the human brain has two primary impulses shaping our behaviour in social situations: the first instinct is to minimise threat, and the second instinct is to maximise reward. In other words, we are hard-wired to survive. Isn't it fascinating that our 3-pounder brain rules how we respond to situations and people depending on whether our brain perceives it as a rewarding situation or a threatening one?

Fundamentally, Rock's viewpoint clarifies the complex processes by which our brains interpret social cues and determine our actions, emphasising the primary impulses that form the foundation of most of our social interactions.

Rock developed the SCARF neuroscience model—Status, Certainty, Autonomy, Relatedness, and Fairness—to capture the fundamental social triggers that influence human behaviour:

1. **S**tatus is the desire for relative importance and recognition within a social context.

2. **C**ertainty is the preference for predictability and assurance in the face of ambiguity.

3. **A**utonomy is the need for control and the ability to influence outcomes.

4. **R**elatedness is the drive for meaningful connections and positive social interactions.

5. **F**airness is the quest for perceived fairness and equity in social exchanges.

## Incorporating Rock's SCARF Model in the Gender-intelligent Coaching Approach

Incorporating David Rock's SCARF model into the gender-intelligent coaching framework is crucial for several reasons. The SCARF model provides women with valuable insights into the complex social dynamics that influence their professional journeys. Women often navigate a labyrinth of social complexities in professional spheres, where concerns related to their status, certainty, autonomy, relatedness, and fairness loom large. For instance, women may face workplace dynamics such as challenges regarding fairness, experiencing discrimination, and the perception that men and women are subjected to different rules. Their status can be challenged because they are treated with different respect than their male colleagues. By leveraging the SCARF model in coaching sessions, women gain a deeper understanding of the underlying social factors impacting their workplace interactions and relationships.

Crucially, familiarity with the nuanced interplay of status, certainty, autonomy, relatedness, and fairness equips women with the tools to engage in social interactions with heightened awareness, resilience, and efficacy. This heightened awareness extends to their emotional landscape, enabling women to navigate both their professional and personal domains with greater emotional self-awareness. This self-awareness, in turn, serves as a cornerstone for informed decision-making, effective stress management, and cultivating resilience in the face of adversity.

In essence, David Rock's SCARF model could be co-opted as a guiding framework for women navigating the complex social terrain of professional environments. Its integration into the gender-intelligent coaching framework underscores a commitment to providing women with a holistic coaching approach that recognises and addresses the multifaceted aspects of their social experiences.

Overall, incorporating neuroscience, such as the SCARF model and the Cuddy power poses into coaching offers powerful insights and skills to assist women in achieving greater success. By combining an understanding of neuroscience with other effective coaching strategies, coaches can support women in reaching their full potential.

In conclusion, this chapter has underscored the critical importance of integrating a diverse array of theoretical foundations into the gender-intelligent coaching framework.

The theoretical pillars of the framework—gender theory, integral coaching, ontological coaching, integral theory, social psychology, motivational and goal attainment theories, and neuroscience— collectively form a robust and adaptable coaching methodology. By intertwining these theories, the gender-intelligent coaching framework supports coaching interventions. It provides a comprehensive lens through which coaches and clients can examine and address various coaching issues, especially those related to gender dynamics.

Gender theory serves as the foundational pillar, highlighting the social constructions of gender and the power imbalances that influence women's experiences. Integrating this theory into coaching practices empowers clients to navigate and challenge societal expectations and biases, fostering a gender-equitable personal and professional growth environment.

James Flaherty's integral coaching and Alan Seiler's ontological coaching approaches further enrich the gender-intelligent coaching framework by emphasising clients' holistic development, considering their language, mood, and body. These approaches advocate for a symbiotic coaching relationship, where both coach and client grow together, reflecting the core values of the gender-intelligent coaching approach.

Ken Wilber's integral theory, with its four-quadrant model, offers a comprehensive framework for understanding the complexities of human experience. This model supports clients in gaining insights into the interconnectedness of their inner world with external factors, promoting a holistic approach to personal development.

The inclusion of social psychology in the gender-intelligent coaching framework emphasises the impact of social contexts and group dynamics on individual thoughts, emotions, and behaviours. This perspective is crucial for understanding how societal norms influence women's experiences and decision-making processes.

Motivational and goal attainment theories, particularly self-determination theory and self-efficacy, address the gendered nature of ambition and motivation. These theories provide valuable insights into how coaches can foster a sense of autonomy, competence, and connectedness in their clients, assisting them in overcoming societal biases and achieving their goals.

**CHAPTER 6**

# THE COACHING TOOLS

Now that we have pinned down the W-O-M-A-N coaching model and the gender-intelligent coaching framework that supports the coaching model, we turn our focus on a key component of offering great coaching: the coaching tools we utilise.

Coaches use coaching tools as resources to facilitate the coaching process and enhance our clients' coaching experiences. These coaching tools assist the coach and client in tracking their development, progress, and actions, pinpointing insights, increasing clients' self-awareness and introspection, improving goal-setting and accountability, and so on. Just like planning a trip where choosing the right tools and gear—whether a map, GPS, spare tyre or snacks—is as critical as knowing where you're going, selecting the right coaching tools is equally important in the coaching process.

## The Coaching Toolbox

Intake and Post-Assessment Forms: For instance, intake and post-assessment forms are crucial for tracking coaching effectiveness.

These forms provide a baseline at the beginning of the coaching relationship and help measure progress at the end. They also offer valuable insights into the client's initial state and the outcomes achieved through coaching.

The Wheel of Life: The "Wheel of Life" is an excellent tool for analysing multiple responsibilities and identifying areas for development to improve one's quality of life. This visual tool assists clients in assessing various aspects of their lives, such as career, family, health, and personal growth, and determining where they need to focus their efforts.

Goal-Setting Workbooks and Time-Tracking Worksheets: Goal-setting and time-tracking worksheets are essential for enabling clients to define and achieve their objectives. These tools assist clients in breaking down their goals into manageable steps and tracking their progress over time.

Reflective Diary Entries and Introspective Journaling: Reflective diary entries and introspective journaling encourage clients to explore their thoughts, emotions, and experiences. These practices promote self-awareness and help clients identify patterns and insights that can inform their coaching journey.

Incisive and Generative Questioning: Incisive and generative questioning are potent techniques for deepening the coaching conversation. These questions challenge clients to think critically about their assumptions and explore new perspectives, leading to greater clarity and insight.

Reframing Exercises: Reframing exercises motivate clients to shift their perspectives on challenging situations. By looking at problems from different angles, clients can uncover new solutions and develop a more positive and proactive mindset.

Strength-Based Assessments and Personality Assessments: Strength-based assessments and personality assessments provide clients with a deeper understanding of their unique talents and traits. These tools empower clients to leverage their strengths and address areas for growth, enhancing their overall effectiveness.

The gender-intelligent coaching toolbox utilises a wide array of coaching tools. In particular, the use of intake assessment forms and post-evaluation forms helps track the effectiveness of coaching. Furthermore, the "Wheel of Life" is an excellent tool for analysing multiple responsibilities and identifying areas for development to improve one's quality of life. Additional coaching tools include goal-setting workbooks, time-tracking worksheets, reframing worksheets, introspective and reflective journaling, generative and incisive questioning, and a wide range of other resources. These coaching tools are essential because they serve as catalysts for our clients to sharpen insights into their polyphonous parts, blind spots, habit loops, overall way of being, internal narratives, emotions, and moods, resulting in a deeper awareness of themselves.

Crucial to the gender-intelligent coaching approach are goal-setting coaching tools. John Whitmore's GROW model, which stands for Goal, Reality, Options, and Will, is a preferred goal-setting tool. The GROW model provides a structured framework for goal attainment by defining the goal clients want to achieve, assessing the existing reality and possibilities to achieve it, and promoting action, accountability, and agency.

The GROW model is utilised as a coaching tool within the milestone and action phases of the W-O-M-A-N coaching model. In the gender-intelligent approach, Whitmore's GROW model is a goal-focused coaching tool rather than a coaching model. The choice to use GROW as a coaching tool instead of a coaching model is based on the reality that coaching clients seek coaching not only to achieve specific goals but also to address existential and complex challenges, often uncertain about their intended path and desired outcomes. Sometimes, goal-setting coaching models lack the depth needed for more reflective work.

In summary, coaching tools for reflection, assessment, and tracking are critical elements of the gender-intelligent coaching intervention. The use of these coaching tools encourages reflection, reveals strengths and areas for improvement, and boosts confidence and motivation. In essence, coaching tools are essential aids to the coaching path, guiding women towards self-discovery, progress, and success.

# FORWARD AND BEYOND - EMBRACING THE FUTURE OF GENDER-INTELLIGENT COACHING

*Successful women are already exceptional. The anatomy of their success is unwavering determination, inherent capability, boundless motivation and profound resilience. The art of illuminating these women's brilliance is the essence of gender-intelligent coaching.*

Rosieda Shabodien
(Executive Coach; Gender-Intelligent Coaching Advocate;
Women's Empowerment Specialist)

So, this is it. One could interpret this as either the conclusion of this book or the beginning of a new chapter. I deliberately chose not to refer to it as the conclusion chapter since books never truly come to an end. They may have a final page, but they never represent the final word on a subject. This principle is also applicable to this book.

My journey began with a quest to get a Master's Degree in Coaching, partly driven by bringing closure to the regret of not finishing a previous master's degree. However, this incomplete master's degree turned into a blessing, as it has motivated me to not only pursue another master's degree but to delve deeply into the tangible effects of patriarchy on women and how coaching can serve as a powerful tool to counteract these effects. This exploration, in turn, led me on a journey to craft a dynamic, gender-intelligent coaching approach and to develop the gender-intelligent coaching framework and the W-O-M-A-N coaching model to drive this coaching approach.

As we've navigated this book together, I've invited you to consider how the coaching profession can best support women. This book reflects my experience of coaching women using the gender-intelligent coaching approach. At its essence, this book advocates for a shift in our coaching paradigm—a shift from the confines of gender-blindness or, worse yet, the reinforcement of patriarchal norms—to the adoption of a gender-intelligent coaching approach that acknowledges that biases and stereotypes create metaphorical roadblocks and impede women's journeys to self-actualisation.

This book aligns with the coaching values of our coaching profession, promoting equality, collaboration, introspection, and supporting individuals to reach their full potential by overcoming internal and external obstacles. Understanding these constraints, such as patriarchy, misogyny, and sexism, is crucial for women's self-actualisation.

The book invites us, as coaches, to be torchbearers of progress, illuminating pathways for women to transcend systemic barriers and reclaim their rightful place in the narrative of success.

Furthermore, it suggests that coaching serves as a tool for women's empowerment, empowering our clients to break free from gender bias and stereotypes. And by doing so, creating a world where everyone has the potential to thrive and succeed. Through this, we can unlock the potential of individuals, organisations, and societies. We pave the path for both genders and men's contributions to illuminate the world.

Ultimately, the overarching goal of the book "What Women Want Coaches to Know: A Gender-Intelligent Coaching Approach" is to encourage all coaches, irrespective of gender, to support women's empowerment and gender equality while breaking free from patriarchal norms to create a more inclusive and thriving world.

# BIBLIOGRAPHY

Ahmed, N., Quinn, S.C., Limaye, R.J. & Khan, S. 2021. From Interpersonal Violence to Institutionalized Discrimination: Documenting and Assessing the Impact of Islamophobia on Muslim Americans. *Journal of Muslim Mental Health*. 15(2). DOI: 10.3998/jmmh.119.

Amazon. 2024. Best Sellers in Business Mentoring & Coaching. Available at: https://www.amazon.com/Best-Sellers-Business-Mentoring-Coaching/zgbs/digital-text/10021498011 [2023, Jan 5].

Appelbaum, S.H., Audet, L. and Miller, J.C., 2003. Gender and leadership? Leadership and gender? A journey through the landscape of theories. *Leadership & Organisation Development Journal*, *24*(1), .43-51. DOI: 10.1108/01437730310457320.

Bain, A. 2020. *Working Women's Cognitive Attributions and Self-Perceptions After Experiences of Subtle Sexism and Internalized Sexism*. Available at: https://scholarworks.lib.csusb.edu/etd/1103 [2024, March 17].

Bandura, A. 1977. Self-efficacy: Toward a unifying theory of behavioral change. *Psychological Review*, 84(2):191–215. DOI: 10.1037/0033-295X.84.2.191.

Batara, M.A., Ngo, J.M., See, K.A. Erasga, D., 2018. Second generation gender bias: The effects of the invisible bias among mid-level women managers. *Asia-Pacific Social Science Review*, *18*(2): 138-151. Available at: https://www.researchgate.net/publication/332154630 [2023, Dec 04].

Belle, D., Tartarilla, A.B., Wapman, M., Schlieber, M. & Mercurio, A.E. 2021. "I can't operate, that boy is my son!": Gender schemas and a classic riddle. *Sex Roles*. 85(10). https://doi.org/10.1007/s11199-020-01211-4.

Betron, M., Bourgeault, I., Manzoor, M., Paulino, E., Steege, R., Thompson, K. & Wuliji, T. 2019. Time for gender-transformative change in the health workforce. *The Lancet*, 393(10171), 25-26 DOI: 10.1016/S0140-6736(19)30208-9.

Bianchi, S.M., Milkie, M.A., Sayer, L.C. and Robinson, J.P., 2000. Is anyone doing the housework? Trends in the gender division of household labor. *Social forces*, *79*(1), 191-228. https://academic.oup.com/sf/article/79/1/191/2233934.

Bond, B.J. 2016. Fairy Godmothers > Robots: The Influence of Televised Gender Stereotypes and Counter-Stereotypes on Girls' Perceptions of STEM. *Bulletin of Science, Technology & Society*. 36(2):91–97. DOI: 10.1177/0270467616655951.

Bonneywell, S. 2017. How a coaching intervention supports the development of female leaders in a global organisation. *International Journal of Evidence Based Coaching and Mentoring, Special Issue* (11). Available at: http://ijebcm.brookes.ac.uk [2023, Jan 5].

Boyatzis, R.E. & Jack, A.I. 2018. The neuroscience of coaching. *Consulting Psychology Journal.* 70(1):11–27. DOI: 10.1037/cpb0000095.

Brescoll, V.L. 2016. Leading with their hearts? How gender stereotypes of emotion lead to biased evaluations of female leaders. *Leadership Quarterly.* 27(3):415–428. DOI: 10.1016/j.leaqua.2016.02.005.

Brock, V. 2009. Professional challenges facing the coaching field from a historical perspective. *International Journal of Coaching in Organisations.* 7(1):27-37. Available at: www.ijco.info.[2024, Jan 5].

Bruckmüller, S., Ryan, M., Haslam, S. & Peters, K. 2013. Ceilings, cliffs and labyrinths: Exploring metaphors for workplace gender discrimination. In M. K. Ryan, & N. R. Branscombe (eds.). *The SAGE Handbook of Gender and Psychology.* SAGE Publications Inc. 450–464. DOI: 10.4135/9781446269930.n27.

Carli, L.L. & Eagly, A.H. 2016. Women face a labyrinth: an examination of metaphors for women leaders. *Gender in Management: An International Journal,* 31(8):514–527. DOI: 10.1108/GM-02-2015-0007.

Carter, A., Sisco, C. & Malik, R. 2022. 'I was exhausted, and there was no break at all': how black women leadership coaches understood and navigated workplace tensions after the racial reckoning. *Philosophy of Coaching An International Journal,* 7(1). DOI: 10.22316/poc/07.1.02.

Catalyst. 2023. *Women's Earnings: The Pay Gap (Quick Take).* Available at: https://www.catalyst.org/research/womens-earnings-the-pay-gap. [2024, May 08].

Clance, P.R. & Imes, S.A. 1978. The imposter phenomenon in high achieving women: Dynamics and therapeutic intervention. *Psychotherapy: Theory, Research & Practice.* 15(3):241–247. DOI: 10.1037/h0086006.

Cuddy, A.J.C., Wilmuth, C.A., Yap, A.J. & Carney, D.R. 2015. Preparatory power posing affects nonverbal presence and job interview performance. *Journal of Applied Psychology,* 100(4). DOI: 10.1037/a0038543.

Cullen, Z. & Perez-Truglia, R. 2023. The Old Boys' Club: Schmoozing and the Gender Gap. *American Economic Review.* 113(7):1703–1740. DOI: 10.1257/aer.20210863.

Deci, E.L. & Ryan, R.M. 2000. The "what" and "why" of goal pursuits: Human needs and the self-determination of behavior. *Psychological Inquiry*, 11(4):227–268. DOI: 10.1207/S15327965PLI1104_01.

Duarte, M., Losleben, K. & Fjørtoft, K. 2023. *Gender Diversity, Equity, And Inclusion In Academia: A Conceptual Framework for Sustainable Transformation*. 1st edition. London: Routledge.

Eagly, A.H. 2005. Achieving relational authenticity in leadership: Does gender matter? *Leadership Quarterly*. 16(3):459–474. DOI: 10.1016/j.leaqua.2005.03.007.

Ely, R.J., Ibarra, H. & Kolb, D.M. 2011. Taking gender into account: Theory and design for women's leadership development programs. *Academy of Management Learning and Education*. 10(3):474–493. DOI: 10.5465/amle.2010.0046.

Equality and Human Rights Commission. 2011. *Sex and Power*. Available at: https://www.equalityhumanrights.com/sites/default/files/sex_and_power_2011_gb_2_.pdf [2024, May 05].

Erskine, S., Brassel, S. and Robotham, K. 2023. Exposé of women's workplace experiences challenges antiracist leaders to step up. Available at: https://www.catalyst.org/reports/antiracism-workplace-leadership. [2024, April 5].

Flaherty, J. 1999. *Coaching-Evoking excellence in others*. Woburn, MA: Butterworth-Heinemann.

Galuk, D. 2009. Executive coaching: what is the experience like for executive women? Available at: https://conservancy.umn.edu/handle/11299/49200 [2019, November 26].

Gilbert, A. & Whittleworth, K. 2009. *The OSCAR Coaching Model*. Monmouthshire: Worth Consulting Pty.

Gladwell, M. 2006. *Blink: The power of thinking without thinking*. Harlow: Penguin Books.

Glick, P. & Fiske, S.T. 2001. An ambivalent alliance: Hostile and benevolent sexism as complementary justifications for gender inequality. *American Psychologist*, 56(2). DOI: 10.1037/0003-066X.56.2.109.

Goldin, C. & Rouse, C. 2000. Orchestrating Impartiality: The Impact of "Blind" Auditions on Female Musicians. *American Economic Review*. 90(4):715–741. DOI: 10.1257/aer.90.4.715.

González, M., Cortina, C. & Rodríguez, J. 2019. The role of gender stereotypes in hiring: A field experiment. *European Sociological Review,* 35(2):187–204. DOI: 10.1093/esr/jcy055.

Gray, J. 1992. *Men are from Mars, women are from Venus : a Practical Guide for Improving Communication and Getting What You Want in Your Relationships.* New York: HarperCollins.

Greig, A. & Flood, M., 2020. Work with men and boys for gender equality: A review of field formation, the evidence base and future directions. *UN-Women Discussion Paper Series. Available at: https://www.unwomen. org [2024, March, 23].*

Hamlin, R.G., Ellinger, A.D. & Beattie, R.S. 2009. Toward a Profession of Coaching? A Definitional Examination of 'Coaching', 'Organisation Development', and 'Human Resource Development'. *International Journal of Evidence Based Coaching and Mentoring,* 7(1):13–38.

Hare-Mustin, R.T. & Marecek, J. 1988. The Meaning of Difference: Gender Theory, Postmodernism, and Psychology. *American Psychologist.* 43 (6): 455-464 https://doi.org/10.1037/0003-066X.43.6.455

Haslam, S. & Ryan, M. 2007. The Glass Cliff: Exploring the Dynamics Surrounding the Appointment of Women To Precarious Leadership Positions. *Academy of Management Review,* 32(2):549–572. DOI: 10.5465/AMR.2007.24351856.

Haynes, M. & Heilman, M. 2013. It Had to Be You (Not Me)!: Women's Attributional Rationalization of Their Contribution to Successful Joint Work Outcomes. *Personality and Social Psychology Bulletin,* 39(7). DOI: 10.1177/0146167213486358.

Heilman, M.E. 2001. Description and prescription: How gender stereotypes prevent women's ascent up the organisational ladder. *Journal of Social Issues,* 57(4). DOI: 10.1111/0022-4537.00234.

Herd, A.M. & Russell, J.E.A. 2010. Tools and techniques: what's in your toolbox? In G. Hernez-Broome, L. A. Boyce, A.I. Kraut (eds.). *Advancing executive coaching.* John Wiley & Sons, Inc. DOI:10.1002/9781118255995. ch10.

Horacek. J. 2020. *Judy Horacek Gender Cartoons.* Facebook, 3 September. Available at:https://web.facebook.com/judyhoracekcartoons/photos/ pb.100063627549267.-2207520000/102005631644846/?type=3 [2023, January 5].

Hunt, J. 2009. Transcending and including our current way of being: An introduction to integral coaching. *Journal of Integral Theory and Practice*, 4(1):1–20.

Ibarra, H., Ely, R. & Kolb, D. 2013. Women rising: The unseen barriers. *Harvard Business Review.* DOI: 10.1063/1.2140612.

International Coaching Federation. 2023. *2023 ICF Global Coaching Study.* Available at: https://coachingfederation.org/app/uploads/2023/04/2023ICFGlobalCoachingStudy_ExecutiveSummary.pdf [2024, January 17].

Inter-Parliamentary Union. 2024. *Global and regional averages of women in national parliaments.* Available at: https://data.ipu.org/women-averages/?date_year=2024&date_month=04 [2024, May 3].

Kahn, M.S. 2014. *Coaching on the Axis: Working with complexity in business and executive coaching.* Randburg: Knowres Publishing (Pty) Ltd.

Kline, P., Rose, E.K. & Walters, C.R. 2022. Systemic Discrimination Among Large U.S. employers. *The Quarterly Journal of Economics*, 137(4):1963–2036. DOI: 10.1093/qje/qjac024.

Koenig, A., Eagly, A., Mitchell, A. & Ristikari, T. 2011. Are leader stereotypes masculine? A meta-analysis of three research paradigms. *Psychological Bulletin*, 137(4). DOI: 10.1037/a0023557.

Körner, R., Petersen, L.E. & Schütz, A. 2021. Do expansive or contractive body postures affect feelings of self-worth? High power poses impact state self-esteem. *Current Psychology*, 40(8):4112–4124. DOI: 10.1007/s12144-019-00371-1.

KR Publishing. 2024. Coaching and Mentoring Books. Available at: https://kr.co.za/kr-library-coaching/

Leimon, A., Moscovici, F. & Goodier, H. 2011. *Coaching women to lead.* New York: Routledge.

Locke, E.A. & Latham, G.P. 2019. The development of goal setting theory: A half century retrospective. *Motivation Science*, 5(2). DOI: 10.1037/mot0000127.

Maher, N. & Hastings, R. 2023. Coaching for gender diversity: A thematic analysis of approaches, frameworks, and their efficacy. *Consulting Psychology Journal*, 75(2):154–175. DOI: 10.1037/cpb0000253.

Mastering Cultural Differences. 2024. *The Gray Ceiling: Unveiling the Impact of Ageism on Women - Part 1*. Available at: https://www.masteringculturaldifferences.com/blog/the-gray-ceiling-unveiling-the-impact-of -ageism-on-women-part-1. [2024, May 08].

Mcleod, A. & Thomas, W. 2010. *The Performance Coaching Toolkit*. Berkshire: Open University Press.

Morgan, M.S. 2017. Glass ceilings and sticky floors drawing new ontologies. In: Chemla, K. & Fox Keller, E., (eds.) *Cultures Without Culturalism in the Making of Scientific Knowledge*. Duke University Press, Durham, US. Available at: http://eprints.lse.ac.uk/65859/ [2023, Dec 23].

Napikoski, L. 2017. *What is a Pink-Collar Ghetto?* Available at: https://www.thoughtco.com/pink-collar-ghetto-meaning-3530822.

Nelson, P. 2018. *There's a Hole in My Sidewalk: The Romance of Self-Discovery*. New York: Atria Books/Beyond Words.

Nuriddin, A., Mooney, G. & White, A.I.R. 2020. Reckoning with histories of medical racism and violence in the USA. *The Lancet,* 396(10256), 949–951. DOI: 10.1016/s0140-6736(20)32032-8.

O'Connor, L.T. & Kmec, J.A. 2020. Is It Discrimination, or Fair and Deserved? How Beliefs about Work, Family, and Gender Shape Recognition of Family Responsibilities Discrimination. *Social Currents*, 7(3):212–230. DOI: 10.1177/2329496519897973.

O'Flaherty, C.M.B. & Everson, J.M.C. 2005. Coaching in Leadership Development. In J. Kagan & A. Böhmert (eds.). *Brain-Based Executive Education*. Johannesburg: Knowres Publishing.

Peery, D., Brown, P. & Letts, E. 2020. *Left Behind and Left Out: The Hurdles, Hassles, and Heartaches of Achieving Long-Term Legal Careers for Women of Color*. Available at: https://www.americanbar.org/content/dam/aba/administrative/women/leftoutleftbehind-int-f-web-061020-003.pdf [2023, April 01].

Porter, E. 2021. Who Discriminates in Hiring? A New Study Can Tell. *New York Times,* 29 July. Available at: https://www.nytimes.com/2021/07/29/business/economy/hiring-racial-discrimination.html [2023, April 01].

Priestly, A. 2023. *Address the 'Double-Glazed Glass Ceiling': Chief Executive Women's Plea to Corporate Australia*. Available at: https://womensagenda.com.au/business/employers/address-the-double-glazed-glass-ceiling-chief-executive-womens-plea-to-corporate-australia/ [2024, May 01].

Ratele, K. & Duncan, N. 2003. *Social Psychology-Identities and Relationships.* Cape Town: Juta and Company.

Richter, S., van Zyl, L.E., Roll, L.C. & Stander, M.W. 2021. Positive Psychological Coaching Tools and Techniques: A Systematic Review and Classification. *Frontiers in Psychiatry*, 12. DOI: 10.3389/fpsyt.2021.667200.

Rippon, G., 2019. *The gendered brain: The new neuroscience that shatters the myth of the female brain.* London: Penguin Random House UK.

Roche, C. & Passmore, J., 2021. Racial justice, equity and belonging in coaching. Henley-on-Thames: Henley Business School.

Rock, D. 2008. SCARF: A brain-based model for collaborating with and influencing others. *NeuroLeadership Journal.* 1(1), 78–87.

Rock, D. 2009. *Managing with the Brain in Mind.* Available at: https://www.psychologytoday.com/sites/default/files/attachments/31881/managingwbraininmind.pdf [2024, April 04].

Ross, A. 2022. There is a coach for that! Oprah Magazine, 2.4, 104.

Ryan, M., Haslam, S., Morgenroth, T., Rink, F., Stoker, J. & Peters, K. 2016. Getting on top of the glass cliff: Reviewing a decade of evidence, explanations, and impact. *Leadership Quarterly,* 27(3):446–455. DOI: 10.1016/j.leaqua.2015.10.008.

Ryan, M.K. & Morgenroth, T. 2024. Why We Should Stop Trying to Fix Women: How Context Shapes and Constrains Women's Career Trajectories. *Annual review of psychology*, 75:555-572. DOI: 10.1146/annurev-psych-032620.

Schulte, B. 2014. 'The Second Shift' at 25: Q & A with Arlie Hochschild. *Washington Post*, 14 August. Available at: https://www.washingtonpost.com/blogs/she-the-people/wp/2014/08/06/the-second-shift-at-25-q-a-with-arlie-hochschild/. [2024, April 04]

Seiler, A. 2003. Coaching to the Human Soul: Ontological Coaching and Deep Change. 1st edition, vol. 1. *Victoria*: Newfield Australia.

Shabodien, R. 2021. The value of executive coaching for women leaders in the NPO sector. Unpublished Master's thesis. MA Philosophy In Management Coaching. Stellenbosch: Stellenbosch University.

Shoukry, H. 2017. Coaching for social change. In T. Bachkirova, G. Spence, & D. Drake (eds.). *The SAGE handbook of coaching. California: Sage Publications, Inc.,* 176-194.

Skinner, S., 2014. Understanding the importance of gender and leader identity formation in executive coaching for senior women. *Coaching: An International Journal of Theory, Research and Practice*, 7(2):102-114. DOI:10.1080/17521882.2014.915864.

Slaughter, A. 2016. *Unfinished Business: Women Men Work Family.* New York: Random House.

Stout-Rostron, S. & Janse Van Rensburg, M. 2012. *Business coaching: Unlocking the secrets of business coaching.* 2nd edition. Randburg: Knowres Publishing (Pty) Ltd.

Stout-Rostron, S. 2014. *Leadership Coaching for Results: Cutting-edge Practices for coach and client.* Randburg: Knowres Publishing (Pty) Ltd.

Swim, J., Aikin, K., Hall, S. & Hunter, B. 1995. Sexism and Racism: Old-Fashioned and Modern Prejudices. *Journal of Personality and Social Psychology*, 68(2):199–214. DOI: 10.1037/0022-3514.68.2.199.

Tahmaseb-McConatha, J., Kumar, V., Magnarelli, J. & Hanna, G. 2023. The Gendered Face of Ageism in the Workplace. *Advances in Social Sciences Research Journal*, 10(1). DOI: 10.14738/assrj.101.13844.

Terblanche, N.H.D., 2020. The coaching model derivation process: combining grounded theory and canonical action research for developing coaching models. *Coaching: An International Journal of Theory, Research and Practice*, 13(1):45–60. DOI: 10.1080/17521882.2019.1619794.

Verniers, C. & Vala, J. 2018. Justifying gender discrimination in the workplace: The mediating role of motherhood myths. *PLOS ONE*, 13(1). DOI:10.1371/journal.pone.0190657.

Vitzthum, C. 2023. A pawn in the game? The significance of contracting in coaching with gender-sensitivity. *International Journal of Evidence Based Coaching and Mentoring*, (Special Issue 17):3–17. DOI: 10.24384/jbdb-xv40.

Whitmore, J. 2017. *Coaching for performance: The principles and practice of coaching and leadership.* [ebook] 5th edition. [Online]. London: John Murray Press. Available at: https://www.bookdepository.com/Coaching-for-Performance-John-Whitmore/9781473658127. [2024, May 08].

Wilber, K. 2011. *A Theory of Everything: An Integral Vision for Business, Politics, Science, And Spirituality.* Boston: Shambhala Publication.

Wilber, K., 2001. *Grace and grit: Spirituality and healing in the life and death of Treya Killam Wilber.* Boston: Shambhala Publications

Young, V. 2011a. *The Secret Thoughts of Successful Women: Why Capable People Suffer from The Impostor Syndrome and How to Thrive In Spite of It.* [Online]. New York: Crown Business

Young, V., 2011b.*The Secret Thoughts of Successful Women: And Men: Why Capable People Suffer from Impostor Syndrome and How to Thrive In Spite of It.* [Online]. New York: Crown Business.

# ENDNOTES

1   Young, 2011.

2   Young, 2011:35.

3   Clance and Imes, 1978.

4   Shoukry 2017.

5   Ryan and Morgenroth, 2024.

6   Stout-Rostron & Janse Van Rensburg, 2012; Kahn, 2014.

7   Shabodien, 2021.

8   Galuk, 2009; Leimon, Moscovici and Goodier, 2011; Skinner, 2014; Bonneywell, 2017.

9   Belle et al.,2021.

10  Koenig et al., 2011.

11  Gladwell, 2006

12  Erskine, Brassel and Robotham, 2023.

13  Ahmed et al., 2021.

14  Koenig et al., 2011.

15  Goldin and Rouse, 2000.

16  Roche and Passmore, 2021.

17  Rippon, 2019.

18  Batara et al., 2018.

19  Betron et al., 2019.

20  IPU, 2024.

21  Catalyst Inc., 2024.

22  Equality and Human Rights Commission, 2011.

23  Heilman, 2001.

24  Heilman, 2001.

25  Gray, 1992.

26  Slaughter, 2016.

27  Bianchi et al., 2000.

28  Greig and Flood, 2020.

29  Bond, 2016.

30  Carli and Eagly, 2016.

31  Peery, Brown & Letts, 2020.

32  Tahmaseb-McConatha et al., 2023.

33  Bruckmüller et al., 2013.

34  Morgan, 2015; Carli and Eagly, 2016.

35  Carli and Eagly, 2016.

36  Napikoski, 2017.
37  Cullen and Perez-Truglia, 2023.
38  Schulte, 2014.
39  Verniers and Vala, 2018.
40  Eagly, 2005.
41  Peery et al., 2020; Priestly, 2023.
42  Haslam and Ryan, 2007; Ryan et al., 2016.
43  Erskine, Brassel and Robotham, 2023.
44  Swim, Aikin, Hall & Hunter, 1995; Ely, Ibarra & Kolb, 2011; Ibarra, Ely & Kolb, 2013.
45  Glick and Fiske, 2001.
46  Duarte, Losleben and Fjørtoft, 2023.
47  Haynes & Heilman, 2013; Bain, 2020.
48  Cullen and Perez-Truglia, 2023.
49  O'Connor and Kmec, 2020; Duarte, Losleben and Fjørtoft, 2023.
50  Catalyst, 2023.
51  Ryan and Morgenroth, 2024.
52  Hamlin, Ellinger and Beattie, 2009.
53  Hamlin, Ellinger and Beattie, 2009.
54  O'Flaherty & Everson, 2005; Brock, 2009.
55  2023 ICF Global Coaching Study, 2023.
56  Ross, 2022.
57  Brock, 2009.
58  Amazon, 2024.
59  KR Publishing, 2024.
60  Roche and Passmore, 2021; Carter, Sisco and Malik, 2022.
61  Roche and Passmore, 2021.
62  Shoukry, 2017.
63  Vitzthum, 2023;Maher and Hastings, 2023.
64  Vitzthum, 2023.
65  Appelbaum, Audet and Miller, 2003; Ely, Ibarra and Kolb, 2011; Ryan and Morgenroth, 2024.
66  Nuriddin , Mooney and White, 2020.
67  Porter, 2021.
68  Kline, Rose and Walters, 2022.
69  González, Cortina and Rodríguez, 2019.
70  Horacek, 2020.
71  Ryan and Morgenroth, 2024.

72  Terblanche, 2020; Richter, van Zyl, Roll & Stander, 2021
73  Terblanche, 2020.
74  Stout-Rostron, 2014; Terblanche, 2020.
75  Herd AM & Russell JEA, 2010.
76  Gilbert and Whittleworth, 2009; Mcleod and Thomas, 2010; Stout-Rostron and Janse Van Rensburg, 2012; Whitmore, 2017.
77  Hare-Mustim & Marecek, 1988.
78  Flaherty, 1999.
79  Seiler, 2003.
80  Hunt, 2009; Wilber, 2011.
81  Ratele and Duncan, 2003.
82  Locke and Latham, 2019.
83  Rock, 2008.
84  Nelson, 2018.
85  Hare-Mustim & Marecek, 1988.
86  Brescoll, 2016.
87  Seiler, 2003.
88  Wilber, 2001.
89  Ratele & Duncan, 2003.
90  Locke and Latham, 2019.
91  Deci and Ryan, 2000.
92  Bandura, 1977.
93  Heilman, 2001; Haynes and Heilman, 2013.
94  Boyatzis & Jack, 2018.
95  Cuddy et al., 2015.
96  Cuddy et al., 2015.
97  Körner, Petersen and Schütz, 2021.
98  Rock, 2008.
99  Rock, 2009, p.3.

# INDEX